IN THE ZONE

Achieving Optimal Performance in Business—as in Sports

Dr. J. Mitchell Perry and Steve Jamison

Library of Congress Cataloging-in-Publication Data

Perry, J. Mitchell, 1951–
    In the zone : achieving optimal performance in business as in sports /
J. Mitchell Perry and Steve Jamison.
       p.   cm.
    ISBN 0-8092-3195-6
    1. Success in business—Psychological aspects.
    2. Sports—Psychological aspects.   I. Jamison, Steve.
    II. Title.
    HF5386.P475   1997
    650.1—dc20

                                  96-32425
                                     CIP

Interior design by Mary Lockwood
Interior illustrations by Peanut Harper

Interior photos by permission of AP/WIDE WORLD PHOTOS, except for photo
on page 64, by Everett Edstrom

15   14   13   12   11   10   9   8   7   6   5   4   3   2   1

For Hayden and Marlowe with love from Dad'n
—J. Mitchell Perry

To my father, Everett Edstrom
—Steve Jamison

IN THE ZONE:

Sports and Business

What I took from my athletic background was extremely useful in business. Winning becomes a habit . . . *rising to the occasion is a practice you build—a mental discipline and a practice you build. All the great ones have it.*

> —DAVID POTTRUCK, former nose tackle, University of Pennsylvania; member, College Wrestling Hall of Fame; and currently, president and COO, Charles Schwab Company; in conversation with Steve Jamison

Contents

PREFACE

by Dr. J. Mitchell Perry

If you ask any sports champion what it takes to achieve and maintain championship status, they will answer "90 percent of it is mental." You have heard that remark often—and it's true—90 percent of it is mental. But what is that mental 90 percent about? And how does it work? And what power does it have in business achievements? The answer? Plenty!

This book is about a process I have discovered to deliberately engineer getting into the Zone—it's the same mental state that sports champions utilize, and I've tested and taught this process in the "Perry Performance Classic" since 1988 with thousands of business professionals around the world.

The results? It works! You can learn how to get into the Zone by design to exponentially optimize your performance in anything—sports, fine arts, sales, management, and public speaking.

My coauthor, Steve Jamison, and I are pleased to present you with effective and easy tools to surge into the Zone, recover when you fall out, and then surge into the Zone again.

Remember when you were a child and you had a blast riding your bicycle with your hands off the handlebars? That's being in the Zone, and this book will show you how to do it often and by design.

May the "Hands-Free Zone" be with you!

PREFACE

by Steve Jamison

If you're an athlete or a sports fan, you're familiar with the term *in the Zone*, often used to describe a player (or team) who suddenly rises to an almost magical level of performance during competition. Announcers also describe that athlete as being "out of his [or her] head," "possessed," "on fire," "in a trance," or "unconscious." When an individual has tapped into, or unleashed, his or her greatest potential, he or she is "in the Zone." Michael Jordan calls it his "fourth gear."

In 1977 professional golfer Al Geiberger reached an astonishing "Zone" or "gear" when he accomplished something unequaled by Ben Hogan, Jack Nicklaus, Arnold Palmer, or anyone else in the history of professional golf. Geiberger shot 59 during the Memphis Open at the formidable Colonial Country Club (7,200 yards). Mr. 59, as he is now called throughout the golf world, told me recently in Palm Springs, California, "The day I shot 59, I didn't know I was in the Zone until I was out of the Zone." Unconscious? Indeed.

In Sports, Business, and Life

Professor Mihaly Csikszentmihalyi, former chairman of the Department of Psychology at the University of Chicago, calls what happened to Geiberger and others *flow* (this term also serves as the title of his excellent book). He describes "flow" as when an individual reaches a state of concentration so intense it amounts to an absolute absorption in a particular activity, regardless of whether its in the context of sports, business, or life.

That state of total absorption in the performance, or process, precludes doubt, anxiety, and fear and produces what is commonly known as *the Zone*, when all distractions fall away and optimum performance ensues. The Zone is a state of mind characterized by self-trust, enjoyment, and focused relaxation. The purpose of this book is to give you the tools to reach this state professionally and personally.

What can be so frustrating about the Zone is that it's an elusive commodity, appearing suddenly and without warning and then vanishing just as quickly. However, high achievers in both sports and business understand that it is not just happenstance.

High achievers know that while the Zone resists being summoned on command, they do have access to the ability to reach within and draw forth a near-optimum (or optimum) performance level and that there is much they can do to facilitate its arrival.

The Ugly Zone

In *Winning Ugly: Mental Warfare in Tennis*, the primary issue my coauthor, Brad Gilbert (Andre Agassi's coach, considered by many to be the world's number-one tennis strategist), and I addressed was how to apply your specific abilities in tennis to maximum advantage against an opponent and how to force the other player to challenge your strengths with his or her weaknesses.

Now, Dr. J. Mitchell Perry, internationally renowned performance consultant, my coauthor of *In the Zone*, and I examine an adversary closer than the player on the other side of the net. We look at the opponent within, namely, you and your mental "technology." We show how most individuals in business beat *themselves* by utilizing learned weaknesses or liabilities instead of their natural strengths.

More important, we give you a step-by-step formula for turning this around so you are capitalizing on your attitudinal and emotional strengths while minimizing or eliminating your conditioned weaknesses.

We show you how to get in (or near) the Zone on a consistent basis, to do your best while at the same time removing much of the stress from your success!

ACKNOWLEDGMENTS

Thanks to Paul Wright for his unfailing support, Toni Boyle for her insight and guidance, Sam Yates for his wisdom, George Smainis for his mentorship, and Faye Goleman for her standards; also Barry Patmore, Jim Andrews, Mike Reasor, Bob Treadway, Henry Lee, and Christine Sepulveda; and especially my children, Marlowe and Hayden.

DR. J. MITCHELL PERRY

Thanks to my parents, Ev and Mary Edstrom; my sisters, Pat, Kris, Kate, and Kim; also Coach John Wooden, Michael Cronen, David Varner, Dr. Julius Colbert, Charlie Boone, Steven Cannon, Ben Ailes, Roy Stark, Coach Bill Walsh, Jeff Perkins, Dr. George Sheehan, David Pottruck, Randy Cross, Teri Gibson, Thomas H. Edstrom, Andre Agassi, Brad Gilbert, Paul Annacone, Roman Genn, Tim and Peanut Louie-Harper, Dick McKegney, and the many others whose insights and experience helped me in the creation of *In the Zone*.

STEVE JAMISON

INTRODUCTION

Life is the same as athletics.
> —ROGER STAUBACH, Dallas Cowboys
> quarterback, two-time Super Bowl
> winner, member NFL Hall of Fame

As parents we seek to have our children participate in sports as part of their early education because we know the knowledge acquired there can be invaluable. Young people learn discipline, dedication, teamwork, individual responsibility, and sacrifice. They learn what it takes to win and how to deal with loss.

For ourselves, however, we tend to view sports principally as a source of entertainment, something to watch rather than to learn from. This shift in perception occurs at our own great expense.

There is much to be learned from sports that has direct application to our professional and personal lives. Golf legend Jack Nicklaus once observed, "Golf is 90 percent mental." Business is even more so. And just as the great achievers in sports are generally regarded as having the most refined mental skills when it comes to meeting and overcoming challenges, the most successful individuals in business also have superior abilities in this area.

It's important to note that many of the mental management techniques, attitudes, and skills used in sports are identical to those used in business. *In the Zone* reveals them and shows how to apply them in your own life.

The Mirror: Past, Present, and Future

In revealing these mental management techniques and attitudes, *In the Zone* may initially resemble an old, dust-covered mirror that reflects a vaguely familiar image. On closer inspection, however, you will notice the reflected image is not of you but of something more elusive, namely, your mind and how it operates under the pressure of trying to obtain top performance results both professionally and personally.

The reflection in that mirror will be familiar because American adults in the business and corporate world are remarkably alike in how they think. Unfortunately, this common mode of thinking is usually counterproductive, creating diminished performance results and decreasing enjoyment over the long term.

This performance-inhibiting thought process is the subject of Part I, "The Opponent," which reveals the adversaries we identify as the Paradox of Performance, Polar Thinking, and your Critical Advisor, foes whose presence stands in the way of optimum performance results.

Part II, "Your Team," examines the dormant strengths and power you have within that have been increasingly neglected over the years. They are the elements you will use for getting back in the Zone. We call these impact players the Power of Hands-Free, the Power of the Process, and the Leverage of Language.

Part III, "Your Game Plan," then provides you with a specific step-by-step mental technology, the Perry Principles, which will enable you to achieve your optimum performance results on a consistent basis, confident, focused, and enjoying the Process.

The Zone

And now let's begin a journey that will bring you greater success, prosperity, and happiness! It is a journey toward unleashing your greatest potential. Welcome to what Michael Jordan calls the "fourth gear." Welcome to the Zone.

STEVE JAMISON
DR. J. MITCHELL PERRY

THE OPPONENT

The Paradox of Performance

Madison Square Garden is packed on this wild night of NBA semifinals play-off action when abruptly the raucous crowd utters a collective gasp—Michael Jordan and Patrick Ewing have collided in midair, and one of them has crashed hard to the court.

The play started when the Bulls' Jordan rolled off a pick set by Scottie Pippen at the top of the key. With a few elegant and powerful strides Jordan became airborne in a bold attempt to jam an embarrassing dunk over Ewing, the muscled and menacing New York Knicks center who desperately seeks an NBA championship title.

Like every self-respecting center in professional basketball, Ewing is violently territorial about the real estate directly in front of, above, and below the metal hoop. He protects it from all intruders, at all costs, at all times, especially during a play-off game when the score is tied with only seconds remaining. Ewing will knock a player on his butt if he is challenged.

Are We Having Fun Yet?

Jordan pays for his effort with a bone-jolting slam into the Garden's polished hardwood floor that shocks even this jaded New York crowd. He lies there motionless while his assailant stares down with his perpetual scowl. Ewing's glowering face seems to say, "Not in *my* house, Jordan. Don't do that in *my* house." The Knicks' big man has done his job.

Air Jordan, stunned and shaken, is tenderly helped to his feet by teammate Pippen while towel boys mop the splattered sweat from the floor. Hands on his hips, Ewing slowly shifts his gaze upward to the Garden's huge overhead monitor and stares at a replay of his harsh work. Ewing's face is that of a predator, one which has just eaten fully. The crowd murmurs again when the replay shows Jordan bouncing off Ewing and clanging down to the wood.

Jordan struggles now to the free throw line slowly, cautiously, as if concerned that something inside might be cracked or broken. Instead of dunking, he has been slam dunked. Instead of scoring, he has been stomped. His face is sweat-drenched and troubled as the referee hands him the ball. He bounces it once, twice, three times as the television camera behind the stanchion zooms in for a close-up. He pauses. The bouncing resumes.

Suddenly on television sets in tens of millions of homes around the world as well the giant twenty-foot monitor suspended from the Garden's ceiling, Air Jordan's visage appears. His expression is changing—from concerned to something else, to a countenance that is calm and relaxed with eyes focused and confident.

Then slowly, almost imperceptibly, the slightest grin appears on the superstar's face. The grin broadens a bit. He just can't help himself, and you know that Michael Jordan must be feeling at this moment of maximum pressure, "This is heaven. I am in heaven."

Are They Having Fun Yet?

Sport, even at its highest and most viciously competitive levels, is still play. Every athlete knows intuitively that when his or her sport becomes work, it is time to leave the game. The athlete will no longer be competitive, and his or her performance will suffer. When the playing field becomes the workplace the athlete knows it's time to get out.

Athletes, especially professional ones, exist in a world that seems to present them with a simple goal. Al Davis,

Even when a championship is at stake, Jordan enjoys his "work."

the irascible owner of the Oakland Raiders, summed it up with a simple directive to his players, "Just win, baby!"

And that is what they are charged with doing under conditions that, short of war, are perhaps more extreme than any others in our society. These include ferocious, relentless, and often violent competition; threat of physical injury (and in rare cases, even paralysis or death); debilitating mental stress; loss of privacy; temptations of the flesh and spirit; and public humiliation. And yet they call it "play."

In fact sport is better than play. For Jordan and his contemporaries it is heaven. Legendary Chicago Bears linebacker Dick Butkus described it as like being in utopia.

Sport is by definition *play* in spite of the cruel pressures it imposes. We *play* ball on the *playing* field. Golf, football, baseball, soccer, tennis, and hockey are all play. We ask one another, "Who *plays* this weekend?" or "Do you know the score of the *game*?" Athletes who retire from their chosen game often describe it as being a kind of death. They must stop playing.

Work Is Work

Meanwhile, in your profession you work. You sell. You manage. You litigate. You advertise. You teach. You organize. You promote. You motivate. You are held accountable, and others are accountable to you. You delegate. But do you play? Unlikely.

In fact, you spend money earned at work to go watch others such as Jordan play. There seems to be little common ground between what you are paid to do professionally and what athletes are compensated for.

And yet you share something very basic with those you pay to see play. Motivated participants in both sports and business have a common core desire—the wish to perform at optimum levels.

Simply put, you strive mightily to do your best in your work just as Air Jordan attempts to do his best in his play. The contexts may be dramatically different, but the goal is exactly the same; specifically, you and the athlete both seek to unleash your greatest potential.

Different Means to an End

However, there is a major difference in the manner and attitude with which you go about achieving your goal and the way in which athletes and coaches such as Jordan, Jack Nicklaus, Joe Montana, Pete Sampras, and others approach obtaining optimum performance levels.

> *I'm a firm believer in the theory that people only do their best at things they truly enjoy. It is difficult to excel at something you don't enjoy.*
> —JACK NICKLAUS

Top athletes understand that ultimately what they do should be enjoyable, even fun, and believe that this pleasurable element is an intrinsic part of obtaining their best results.

You, on the other hand, have a considerably different perception of what it takes to do your best professionally. As one Fortune 500 executive explained to us with certainty, "Fun is not part of my job description." Mr. Nicklaus is right; Mr. Executive is wrong.

The Paradox Defined: What You Know Versus What You Do

We can prove that people do their best at things they enjoy by examining what you know empirically about your own performance results at work and elsewhere. In those instances when you do your absolute best, when suddenly the process you are engaged in brings forth your finest efforts, certain attitudes or conditions are usually present. This holds whether it's a sales presentation, a keynote speech, a strategy meeting with your department heads, a meeting with your company's CEO, or a four-foot putt that wins you twenty dollars on Saturday morning.

When you reach optimum performance levels (i.e., do your best) you would probably describe yourself as enjoying the process. While very focused on the task, you're also free from anxiety, relatively relaxed. You would also note that in a situation of top personal performance there is total self-trust, confidence in your abilities.

To put it another way, you know that in those important moments of selling, negotiating, promoting, organizing, public speaking, or anything else, it is exponentially more difficult to accomplish your goal if you dislike the experience, have your focus diverted to something other than the task at hand, are filled with anxiety and doubt, and lack self-confidence.

In your gut your understand that when you're really rolling it's effortless, smooth, and fun. You're having a blast. That's when you nail it, when your inner potential is suddenly your outer reality. You're in the Zone.

Thus, the following four conditions are generally present when you are achieving your best performance results:

1. Enjoyment—you're having a blast!
2. Focus—you have keen awareness and alertness

3. Relaxation—you're free from extreme anxiety
4. Self-trust—you have confidence in your judgment

We Are Taught the Opposite

However, what we are taught and conditioned to believe from an early age about doing our best in life, achieving optimum performance, is the opposite. From the moment our education at home and in school begins we are instructed by word and deed that to do well we must work; to do better and better we must work harder and harder. It's part of the promise of the American Dream, which tells us "Work hard and you can have the good life." The paradox lies in our societal perception and definition of *work*.

Webster's defines it very accurately for most for us. *Work* is synonymous with *labor, toil, grind*. Work is an obligation requiring sacrifice and self-denial. Fun? Play? Enjoyment? All are absent in the *Webster's* definition and probably in yours.

We learn that the conditions associated with work are the opposite of those associated with play. We may even vaguely believe that the more miserable we are, the harder we must be working.

Headline: Executive Dies of Heart Attack at 52: Big Success

A *workhorse* is someone who "burns the midnight oil," knows that "nothing good comes easy," and is valued for that effort and philosophy. A dedicated executive can be identified by the furrowed brow, clenched jaw, and stern demeanor as well as the high blood pressure, ulcers, and insomnia. The dedicated executive's motto is "OK, enough fun. Let's get back to work." That executive even wears his or her pain like a badge. The message? Enjoyment and work are mutually exclusive.

Work is labor, and the workplace is commonly referred to as the "salt mine," where you "buckle down," "keep your nose to the grindstone," and "put your shoulder to the wheel." You wait for "hump day" and then for Friday when you visit a restaurant called T.G.I. Friday's, which markets the enjoyment of food and drink in an ambience associated with the joy of surviving five hard days of work. As the old saying goes, "Life is hard, and then you die." By *life* they mean *work*.

Equally important, even if you generally enjoy what you do professionally, those circumstances where you perceive the stakes as high or where the situation makes you uncomfortable (e.g., being selected to deliver the keynote address at the annual convention or asking the boss for a promotion) can become something almost torturous, namely, work, and you can't wait until it's over.

Review the Paradox

Thus, what we know in our gut about the conditions—enjoyment, focused relaxation, and self-trust—that bring forth our own best performance is contrary to what we have been taught to do, namely, suffer!

We define work in pejorative terms to such an extent that we question that which is obtained too easily and without great pain. We think, "This can't last," "It's too good to be true," "What's the catch?", "I shouldn't be enjoying myself," or, most telling of all, "I shouldn't be getting paid for this!"

The latter is damning evidence about our learned perception of work. Why should enjoyment and employment be mutually exclusive? Because it doesn't jibe with the societal perception that holds that if it's enjoyable it can't be work and we shouldn't get paid (unless we are professional athletes!).

We associate work with discomfort, deprivation, even pain because we believe that sweat is good. Sweat can be good, but few individuals recognize when they've gone too far and created their own personal sweatshop. They cross over from being productive to working in a manner that is counterproductive—stressed out, full of self-doubt, and miserable.

Most of the time when executives say they should be working harder, they are wrong. They should be working "easier," taking much of the pain, stress, consternation, anxiety, and "work" out of work.

Pain Adds Value

"No pain, no gain" became a catchphrase because it corresponded with our belief that if something doesn't hurt, its worth or effectiveness is questionable. For example, original Listerine was marketed in a medicinal bottle, and its extremely unpleasant taste was extolled. The advertising experts knew the public's interpretation of this would be "It looks bad and tastes terrible. This stuff must work."

Pain is good. Pain adds value. Pain works. One famous fitness guru urged us to "feel the burn" when exercising. Only later did doctors warn us that we might be better off to simply stop when it burns or we could hurt something. As noted stress and motivational health expert Kris Edstrom tells clients, "No pain, no gain—insane!"

We have been conditioned to accept as normal, even preferable, that which is negative, painful, and counterproductive. Enjoyment is suspect. Play is trivialized. Pain is preferable. How did this happen?

There are contemporary and historical explanations as to why our perception of work is so negative. Here's a brief glance at how it started.

A Painless History of Pain

Americans have always had a side to us that eschewed pleasure and frivolous enjoyment. We can blame some of it on our founding fathers.

> *Do you know why we're so uptight in*
> *America? Because the Puritans came here and*
> *the really fun people all stayed behind.*
> —ROSANNE BARR

With all due respect to our Puritan predecessors, they did have an exceedingly stern approach to living and working. Those attitudes became part of the perception of who we are and what constitutes work in America. You may remember learning about the Protestant work ethic in high school.

The Puritans, Calvinists, and others of equally grim demeanor did not countenance frivolity or casual fun, especially in the context of work. At one point they even made Christmas *illegal*.

It has been suggested that the Puritans outlawed bear-baiting not because it was gruesome torture to bears, but because they were opposed to the enjoyment it afforded spectators. H. L. Mencken defined Puritanism as "the haunting fear that someone, somewhere, may be happy." Had cable television existed in 1623 we can assume with some degree of certainty there would have been very few Puritan households subscribing to the Comedy Channel.

Theirs was a philosophy of righteous self-denial, abstinence, and hard work that was part of one's offering to God. They gave religious sanction to the business enterprise and in doing so united God and mammon.

So, in fairness to the Puritans they must be given much credit for creating the American view that making money is something righteous—just don't have fun in the Process (more on *Process* in Chapter 5).

To the Puritans business was essentially done in the name of God, and thus work was almost religious in nature. Subsequently, a large part of our American tradition reveres hard work, that which is gained through "the sweat of one's brow" and requires great effort. Work is work and should hurt. That concept is a fundamental, pervasive, and profound part of the contemporary view of work in the American psyche.

First the Puritans, Then Our Parents

Add to the Puritans' view of work the fact that parents teach kids that work and play are separate areas of life. Kids are born to have fun and can do it in almost any circumstance. Parents "understand" that fun and (home) work are mutually exclusive and attempt to stamp out traces of the former whenever the latter is present.

Thus, when we were kids doing homework our parents spent a great deal of their time telling us "Quit fooling around; finish your homework," "Pay attention," "Be serious," "You can't go out and *play* until you do your home-*work*."

Enjoyment Enhances Education

Only the most enlightened and creative parents and educators successfully make learning enjoyable for kids. They understand that enjoyment is an enormous catalyst for doing well. They realize that making education as painful as punishment is counterproductive. The same principle holds true in our professions.

Thus, early on we begin to separate in our minds the concepts of *work* and *play*. They become identified as separate and opposing activities. The best proof of this may be our own approach to dealing with our children in these areas.

And so, as we mature and enter the workforce we use as a model for what constitutes the appropriate and most productive attitude a mindset that is, in fact, counterproductive to optimum performance.

What all of this produces in corporate America (as well as industrial America) is a work ethic that is a formula for inducing suboptimum performance results from both individuals and organizations. The manner in which we perceive work sanctions anxiety and stress, makes us distrustful of enjoyment, and reduces self-confidence.

To work hard is to push ourselves past enjoyment and maximum results to a point of anxiety, stress, irritability, and pain both for us and those around us. In fact, as already noted, being stressed out is how we commonly identify that we are working and being productive.

The Perspective in Sports

High achievers in the world of sports have dramatically different expectations and attitudes, ones that foster optimum individual and team results. The smile that appeared on Jordan's face at a critical moment in a play-off game reflects that difference.

An even more dramatic and to some, incomprehensible, example occurred in the finals of the 1996 French Open between Steffi Graf and Arantxa Sanchez Vicario. In addition to the enormous pressure of playing for the championship, additional stress factors were present.

For Graf the match had historical significance. A victory on the red clay courts of Roland Garros Stadium would give her her nineteenth Grand Slam singles title, putting her in second place on the all-time list of champions (behind Helen Wills Moody but ahead of contemporaries Chris Evert and Martina Navratilova).

Sanchez Vicario needed a win in the French Open to reestablish her presence after an eighteen-month decline in her previously booming tennis career. Both competitors had a ferocious desire for victory in what became a brutal test of mental and physical skills. It made what occurred near the end of the grueling match extremely revealing.

A Case of the Giggles

After splitting the first two sets, Graf and Sanchez Vicario were battling deep in the third when suddenly the usually stoic German began giggling during a changeover. Then it continued briefly out on the court. At a moment when anxiety, exhaustion, nerves, fear, or anger might have been expected, Graf had a mini laughing fit near the end of this record-setting three-hour-and-three-minute contest.

Why? Graf's explanation was direct. "I was just having so much fun out there," she said. She, like Jordan, simply loved playing, even under extreme pressure. Graf won the match and the championship 6–3, 6–7(4), and 10–8 in one of the greatest finals ever played in women's tennis, a pressure-packed contest that for Graf was first and foremost *play*.

This attitude exhibited by Jordan, Graf, and others mentioned in the following chapters is one you can bring into your own professional experience. As we progress through *In the Zone* you will learn how to take much of the pain out of work and replace it with enjoyment, focused relaxation, and self-trust.

POLAR THINKING

The Curse of the Contest

Americans love a winner and hate a loser.
They loathe the very thought of losing.
—GEORGE C. SCOTT as General George
Patton in the movie *Patton*

In America the biggest question is usually "Who's number one?" We live in a scorecard society with a contest mentality where the predominant criterion is victory and the most grievous sin is failure. Unfortunately, over the past forty-five years our definition of what constitutes failure has expanded to include virtually everything other than first place, number one, the gold medal.

While coming in second *is* last place in Patton's World War II scenario, contemporary society applies this stringent standard to everything from cars to candy bars, from sports competition to business. As you'll see, this standard creates a perspective, a way of framing events, that virtually guarantees the presence of the negative emotions (extreme stress, anxiety, and doubt) identified in Chapter 1 as being extremely counterproductive to your performance potential.

In America success is now equated with victory, and we believe that doing well means beating someone else. *I win* means *You lose*, and the pressure to just win has radically altered our outlook. The culture is suffused with messages that subtly and not so subtly reinforce this concept. A great deal of these messages come from the media's dramatization of what happens in the world of sports.

Losing the Super Bowl is worse than death.
You have to get up the next morning.
—GEORGE ALLEN, Washington Redskins
coach and Super Bowl loser

The Buffalo Bills' head coach Marv Levy, the Denver Broncos' former head coach Dan Reeves, and the Minnesota Vikings' former head coach Bud Grant all understand how harsh our perception of what constitutes winning and losing has become. Each has taken his team to professional football's greatest event, the Super Bowl, on four different occasions (twelve separate appearances) and failed to win. In spite of the fact that cumulatively these men coached teams that appeared in nearly half of all the Super Bowl games ever played, their inability to bring home a winner in that venue brought them a level of ignominy that casts a shadow on their otherwise outstanding careers.

All three have been somewhat tainted because of that failure, perceived as losers because of their inability to win the Big One. A comedian once observed, "It's just their bad luck that at least two of them couldn't have faced *each other* in the Super Bowl. That way one guy could have gotten the monkey off his back." That monkey appeared, of course, in part because these men are in the rarefied group of coaches brilliant enough to get to the Super Bowl four times apiece.

Thus, Levy, Reeves, and Grant are plagued by the ironic question, "Why didn't you win?" when they are actually among pro football's most successful and winningest coaches.

The question is additionally inappropriate because there are eleven NFL teams that have not been to a *single* Super Bowl contest and a great many more NFL coaches who have attended the event only as spectators sitting in the stands holding a hot dog. What are *they* if Levy, Reeves, and Grant are considered to be somehow flawed? Our skewed contest mentality lumps them all together as losers of varying kinds and degrees.

Perhaps Al Davis misstated the concept with his bold "Just win, baby!" exhortation. In fact, he (and others) meant "Never lose, baby, never lose!" Below winning, there is only darkness.

All or Nothing

> *I must win. I must always win. I cannot be number two.*
> —ARNOLD KOPELSON, producer of *The Fugitive*, *Platoon*, and other movies

Our scorecard, or contest, mentality obviously is applied to much more than football or sports in general. *U.S.A. Today* and other publications list on a weekly or daily basis the number-one television show, video rental, record album, movie, soap opera, concert attraction, news broadcast, television network, book, and automobile. The top colleges, grad schools, medical schools, and prep schools are ranked in descending order.

Media coverage of political campaigns overwhelmingly focuses on who's winning the race at the expense of substantive information about a candidate's policy positions except as to how those positions might affect their standings in the contest.

Fortune 500 annually lists the richest individuals, largest corporations, and top ten stocks in the country. *U.S.A. Today* even catalogs the number-one-selling candy bar in America (Snickers, last time we checked).

Polar Thinking: The Two-Option Trap

The result, or curse, of this contest mentality that permeates our society is that adults in America are conditioned to interpret all situations (especially those in business) as having just two possible options or results. We call this mentality *polar thinking*, and it is the "curse of the contest." It is so powerful, so universal, so seductive that it never occurs to us that we even do it.

Two-option Polar Thinking is reflexive analysis that distills potential results into two diametrically opposed possibilities: win or lose (see Kopelson quote previous), victory or defeat, life or death, right or wrong, all or nothing, black or white, thin or fat, me or you, us or them, smart or stupid, my way or the highway, and the list goes on.

Some adults practice Polar Thinking habitually while others do it selectively, in those situations where the stakes are perceived as high and where it can do the most damage.

At this point you should protest, "Wait a minute! I want to win. Nobody remembers who came in second. If *I* don't win, *you* do, right? And I don't want you to win. I want me to win. Life is win or lose!" Your basic assumption is correct. For the record, winning is great!

This book is all about winning, achievement, and taking a lot of the stress out of success. However, two-option Polar Thinking greatly reduces your ability to achieve results by creating an internal environment that inhibits optimum performance. Polar Thinking does this by presenting you with just two possibilities, one of which is disastrous (e.g., win or *lose*). When this happens the mind automatically tightens and produces doubt, anxiety, and fear—pain! And, as noted in Chapter 1, "The Paradox of Performance," you interpret this pain as a positive sign, a sign of productivity, when in fact it is extremely counterproductive.

Indeed, two-option Polar Thinking has created an increasingly common anomaly in America, the winner who is miserable.

No Joy for Troy

[Dallas quarterback Troy] Aikman finds he
still isn't having much fun.

The news service trumpeted this headline immediately following Dallas's victory in Super Bowl XXX. (Note that the name Super Bowl and the use of Roman numerals are intentionally used to bestow great import on the event. If it were called the thirtieth NFL Championship Game, it would not evoke the same dramatic Roman gladiatorial imagery and exemplify the ultimate in Polar Thinking, I live—you die.)

The Aikman story detailed how participating in and winning Super Bowls had become less and less enjoyable for the future Hall of Famer. His words of celebration following his team's victory over the Pittsburgh Steelers on January 29, 1996, were "I guess it's a feeling more of relief than anything else."

Observers noted that Aikman had gone from being "ecstatic" after his first Super Bowl win to being "happy" following his second Super Bowl victory in 1994. In 1996? He felt simply relief that the whole thing was over. "I don't know," he said, "maybe there has just been so much expected of the football team."

His teammates shared this view. The *New York Times* reported, "A peek around the Cowboys postgame locker room on Sunday night revealed a team that looked as if it was more relieved than it was exhilarated over winning football's world championship."

Both Aikman and his teammates were relieved because they had managed to fulfill the Polar Thinking expectations of others (including owner Jerry Jones), many of whom had little idea how enormous the obstacles had been

Polar Thinking destroyed Aikman's joy of winning.

or how hellish the struggle had become with loss of key players through trades, free agency, and injuries. Aikman and his teammates knew they didn't have a lock on anything and that anyone who thought otherwise was uninformed.

Nevertheless, the Dallas players unwittingly accepted the outside assumptions and expectations and were subsequently left to perform their tasks in a cauldron of pressurized Polar Thinking—win or die!

At a moment when these athletes could have been filled with joy many of them were joyless. Polar Thinking had infected their outlook. They felt relief simply because in their collective mind they had been spared, hadn't suffered the athletic equivalent of death. Did they win because of Polar Thinking? No. They won in spite of the unnecessary counterproductive pressure it created.

And Polar Thinking had certainly robbed them of one of the great rewards of victory, namely, the joy of winning. Consider how irrational it is for someone to describe victory in the Super Bowl as being simply a relief.

Coach Wooden Walks Away from Polar Thinking

Legendary UCLA basketball coach John Wooden also had firsthand experience with Polar Thinking, and it played a role in his own decision to retire. While he resisted Polar Thinking himself, he saw it increasingly exhibited by spectators, fans, and journalists who came to believe that unless UCLA repeated the phenomenal task of winning a national championship each year, the season had been a failure.

This was demonstrated most noticeably in 1975 immediately after Wooden's team won its tenth NCAA Division I championship in twelve years. (The previous season UCLA had lost in the semis to North Carolina State.) After outscoring Kentucky 92–85 in the championship game at the San Diego Sports Arena, Wooden started walking though the noisy crowd toward the dressing room. As reporters, fans, and photographers crowded around him, a loyal UCLA supporter, a man he recognized and knew, ran up to him in a congratulatory mood and said, "Great win, Coach Wooden, especially after the way you let us down last year!"

While Coach Wooden was virtually a Zen master at staying in the process, of removing concern for the outcome from his consciousness, his unprecedented success had distorted the perspective of outsiders. Polar Thinking was the device they now used to measure performance and results: win a national championship or you're a loser! There were many reasons for Coach Wooden's retirement, but cultural Polar Thinking had certainly played some part in taking the joy out of winning for the world's most successful coach. That game would mark his final appearance as a coach.

Number-One Boris Becker Self-Destructs

Three-time Wimbledon champion Boris Becker, a ferocious competitor, described the depressing effect the perceived demands of becoming and remaining number one in the world had on him saying "To play as if your life were to end at the end of a match, with no morning after . . . is devastating." Becker existed in a world where there was no second place, win or die.

After some initial euphoria with achieving the world's number-one ranking, the German tennis star experienced a deep depression that he described as almost self-destructive. "You fall into a black hole, as happened to me after the U.S. Open and Wimbledon [championships]. I am afraid of that hole." Polar Thinking created that hole for Becker even in victory and eventually contributed to future losses.

The Shark Attacks Himself

Greg Norman, golf's Great White Shark, has been affected by Polar Thinking in his own way. Since second place was equivalent to last place (especially in the Majors) Norman put enormous and often debilitating pressure on himself in tournaments where he was still in the hunt on the final day.

In 1986 Norman led all four Majors going into the final round, something that had never been accomplished before, but was victorious in only the British Open. In fact, during his career he has held the lead going into the final day seven times in Majors and produced only one victory. This brought forth some questions regarding his fragility under pressure. Norman *was* susceptible to pressure, the destructive pressure of Polar Thinking.

His all-consuming desire to win made him overly aggressive, subject to poor decision making at crucial times and occasional physical malfunction. Because of Polar Thinking he was trying too hard. Golf's acerbic analyst Gary McCord described it vividly by suggesting that Norman wanted to win so badly he "got 'psycho-cramps' and imploded."

Then in the first half of the 1990s, the Great White Shark seemed to have adjusted his perspective. While retaining an enormous appetite for victory in the Majors (especially the Masters), according to McCord, he was "trying not to focus too hard" on that goal. As sports psychologist Richard Coop advised, "Quit trying to make yourself win, and just let it happen."

In other words, Norman seemed to be controlling his Polar Thinking and was Golfer of the Year in 1995. And then, unexpectedly, Polar Thinking engulfed him again during the 1996 Masters and created one of the most spectacular "chokes" in the history of sports.

The Shark Drowns in Polar Thinking

Norman's opening round at Augusta was a course-record-tying 63, which he then followed with rounds of 69 and 71. After three superb days on a ferociously difficult course, Norman was thirteen strokes under par with a six-shot lead over his nearest rival, Nick Faldo. It appeared Norman was a cinch to stroll to victory and finally claim his coveted Masters trophy on Sunday. As he prepared to leave the clubhouse after his Saturday round, an acquaintance even approached him saying, "Greg, old boy, there's no way you can @*%# this up now!" in reference to past failures.

It made sense to an outsider. After all, no man had ever blown a six-stroke lead going into the final round of a Majors tournament. ESPN's Dan Patrick announced that if Norman lost on Sunday it would be "the biggest collapse in golf history." Add to this external dialogue whatever thoughts rattled around Norman's head Saturday night and Sunday morning and you have the quintessential example of Polar Thinking's rising up and poisoning one's thought process and subsequent performance. Win or die, Greg Norman! And he died.

> *Handling pressure is the difference between winning and losing.*
> —RAY FLOYD, golfer

Polar Thinking sinks the Shark.

From the very first shot of the final round (an ugly, hooked drive) Norman evidenced the fear, the choking, the pressure that Polar Thinking creates with its do-or-die scenario. His swing looked subtly different; his preshot routine became longer and longer, as if he were afraid to pull the trigger; and eventually you could even discern the fear in his eyes when the camera zoomed in for a close-up. His stroll to victory had become a crawl into hell as he buckled under the weight of Polar Thinking.

Norman lost to Nick Faldo by five strokes and joined the ranks of those who are sent to a special kind of sports purgatory reserved for those who succumb to the ravages of extreme Polar Thinking.

Two-Option Polar Thinking Hurts All

Troy Aikman's Cowboys won in spite of Polar Thinking, but the joy of victory was stolen from them. John Wooden saw the "Just win [all the time], baby" climate created by the press and public. Boris Becker cost himself future Grand Slam titles and diminished his performance for several years because he had been drawn into the win-lose paradigm of Polar Thinking. Greg Norman craved first place in the Majors to such a degree that he exuded palpable tension and would often self-destruct when the match was on the line.

Palpable tension is a by-product of Polar Thinking. Thinking "Gotta win," is as destructive as thinking "Don't lose," "Don't fail," or "Don't look stupid." Greg Norman, like so many others, had been subject to both extremes. Unfortunately for him the results have occurred in the most highly visible circumstances.

Capalbo's Circle of Excellence

Just as top athletes and coaches are susceptible to two-option Polar Thinking, successful executives bring it into their corporate environment to the detriment of themselves and their associates.

Richard Capalbo, a successful Merrill Lynch executive in southern California, is a hard-driving sales leader with extremely high standards of performance, for both himself and those who work with him. Capalbo has graying hair and a slight paunch from long hours and too little exercise. His furrowed brow reveals an individual who takes his job seriously.

Capalbo joined us at the Silverado Country Club in California's beautiful Napa Valley for the "Perry Performance Classic," a three-day seminar that uses golf to teach participants about the relationship between how they think and how they perform in business and life. A great deal of this seminar focuses on Polar Thinking.

Golf provides a wonderful opportunity for you to examine the way you think because it exposes two-option Polar Thinking so clearly. Ben Crenshaw, perhaps the world's greatest putter, addressed this when he revealed a very simple but effective practice technique. "I putt better without a hole [in front of him]. Every putt is smooth. Every putt you hit is solid." Crenshaw understood why this is an effective means of practicing a smooth putting motion. In the absence of a hole, Polar Thinking is hard-pressed to construct a success-failure format with its resultant tension and anxiety. Without the win-lose pressure of trying to put the ball in the cup, Crenshaw understood you can concentrate simply on the purity of the stroke itself before Polar Thinking begins to interfere with the stroke's mechanics by introducing doubt, anxiety, and fear ("Will I make it . . . or miss it?").

You Versus You

Golf is a good opportunity for examining the way you think because in golf it is just you against yourself. You may have noticed that business is much like this also. Deadlines, presentations, speeches, selling, and much else come down simply to the level of performance you are able to bring out of yourself.

For a recreational golfer Polar Thinking reveals itself constantly. Richard Capalbo soon recognized his tendency to view his performance in the harsh win-lose framework of Polar Thinking, to value only a perfect shot and to dismiss and be agitated by all others (with his handicap of twelve there were a limited number of perfect shots).

Capalbo gradually began to see that his anger, frustration, pessimism, self-criticism, and lack of self-support after each "bad" shot were extremely counterproductive, often adversely affecting his next shot and the shot after that. Additionally, it also made a round of golf unpleasant for him and anyone in the foursome.

Expanding the Circle of Excellence

More important, Capalbo came to realize that his attitude on the golf course resembled his approach in the corporate environment, but there it had more costly results. "When it came to sales quotas I acknowledged and valued only my super achievers [i.e., those who made the corporate version of the perfect shot]," he explained. "If you didn't give me 110 percent of what you were asked to deliver, I excluded you from my circle of excellence. You were almost invisible." And he offered the same range of nonsupportive and counterproductive responses to those "invisible" associates that he gave himself while playing golf.

His "circle of excellence" was a form of two-option Polar Thinking. You were a super achiever or you were undeserving of recognition and support, all or nothing. Capalbo's perspective on the golf course was, "I hit the ball 225 yards dead straight or I stink"; at Merrill Lynch, "give 110 percent or you stink!"

He declared during conversations, "I want to widen my circle of excellence, of achievement, to offer support, positive input, and communication to people other than the super achiever." He understood the deleterious nature of Polar Thinking both on the golf course and in the conference room.

In the future Capalbo wanted to be both congratulating super achievers and creating them by expanding his circle of excellence and nurturing and supporting effort and achievement at more levels. This he accomplished by recognizing and then eliminating Polar Thinking.

At last report he was quite successful at mastering the issue professionally, less so on the links. But, as master golf course architect Pete Dye maintains, "Golfers love to suffer."

And just as Dye is correct about golfers and suffering, it is also true for most executives and businessmen. We accept the Curse of the Contest, namely, the pain of Polar Thinking, because the Paradox of Performance assures us that when we feel pain we are really working hard and being productive. Polar Thinking supplies an immediate and ongoing source of pain. It is a vicious and counterproductive cycle. Believing that pain signifies productivity, we unknowingly accept a format, two-option Polar Thinking, that is guaranteed to cause that pain.

What About You?

Looming fourth-quarter sales quotas can produce the same misery for you that a six-point deficit in the Super Bowl can produce for Troy Aikman. Your own two-option Polar Thinking predisposes you to fret about the bottom line, the score, success or failure, and victory or defeat; it inhibits your performance potential and enjoyment just as it did for Aikman, Becker, Norman, Capalbo, and many, many others.

Polar Thinking is pervasive in mental calculations both for personal and professional matters and will make you a wreck. It is unproductive and immobilizes and demoralizes you at those times when you need to be strong, confident, energized, and inspired.

3

Your Critical Advisor

The Enemy Within

If I had to do it over again, I wouldn't beat myself up so much.
      —GARDNER DICKENSON, pro golfer

When Michael Jordan ended his stint as a minor-league outfielder for the Chicago White Sox and returned to the Bulls midway through the 1995 season, fans and reporters immediately began speculating about whether he would still be the overpowering force he was when the Bulls won three consecutive NBA titles. After a year and a half away from the game was he still the greatest?

The answer soon became apparent: no. In his first game back Air Jordan was grounded by the Indiana Pacers. He scored only nineteen points and missed shot after shot in a 103–96 loss. It appeared the time off may have diminished his court awareness and perhaps even cost him a step. More disturbing to fans was his relative lack of subsequent improvement. Jordan was still great. He just was not the greatest, no longer the Man.

However, one thing remained undiminished in Jordan's arsenal, his absolute refusal to doubt himself. The Bulls managed to make the play-offs in 1995 and faced an Orlando Magic team that included All-Pro Anfernee Hardaway and All-World center, Shaquille O'Neal, in the Eastern Conference semifinals.

When the Bulls fell behind 3–2 in the series, speculation was rampant that when the Magic won the Eastern Conference semis Chicago would be not only eliminated but virtually eradicated. "Will [Scottie] Pippen demand a trade?" read one headline. Another declared, "Bulls desperate!"; still another, "Bulls don't have the horses." Reporters worked themselves into a frenzy wondering whether Jordan might retire again and prodded him continually to address the troubles he was experiencing.

His response on May 17, 1995, following the Bulls' loss in Game 5, revealed the essence of what Michael Jordan and other optimum performers are all about because it went to the core of his mental technology, the way he thinks. "Everybody's wondering all that stuff right now, but the door's not closed yet. I've been here before. I will not focus on the negative the way many people do." The Bulls eventually did lose to Miami (who in turn lost in the finals to the Houston Rockets), but Jordan believed fully in himself throughout the painful season.

His capacity to resist self-doubt was intact and sparkling (win *or* lose) in spite of the layoff and in spite of the tremendous pressure being exerted on him. Unlike Troy Aikman in 1996, Air Jordan resisted the Polar Thinking expectations and standards of others. Jordan answered only to Jordan—period!

This brings us to the subject of the Critical Advisor. You have one. Jordan doesn't.

A Loaded Pistol Pointed at Your Dreams

There is a latent and insidious voice within each of us called the Critical Advisor. It becomes a loaded pistol that we unconsciously use to intimidate, diminish, and threaten ourselves. Ultimately we can be held hostage by this inner presence at the expense of our personal initiative, creativity, and optimum performance. Did we mention enjoyment? The Critical Advisor destroys enjoyment. It was the Critical Advisor that beat up golfer Gardner Dickenson (see the quote at the beginning of the chapter).

Common Sense Versus the Critical Advisor

The Critical Advisor has its origins in our natural internal Risk-Reward Guidance System, which evaluates the possible results of decisions and future actions. This reasoning ability of ours is usually called *common sense* and is obviously essential to our success (not to mention helping us to decide when to walk across a busy street). Parents would probably agree that teenagers are somewhat lacking in this trait, but gradually most of us develop an effective Risk-Reward Guidance System—prudence and common sense.

"How fast should I drive on this slippery road?" "Is this mutual fund a solid investment?" "Is now the time to try and close this sale?" and thousands of other questions demanding evaluation, decision, and action are analyzed by your inner Risk-Reward Guidance System as it weighs the multiple options and possible outcomes and alternatives.

Over the years this vibrant and productive internal guidance mechanism can become unhealthy and out of balance. As we experience a few personal and professional bumps and bruises along the way, we begin to view situations and ourselves in a manner that is less than supportive and positive.

While Michael Jordan refused to focus on the negative, your Critical Advisor begins focusing more and more on the negative. It becomes your voice of doubt and gives supporting evidence to that negative perspective with large doses of self-doubt, self-criticism, self-disapproval, self-recrimination, self-consciousness, and even self-loathing ("I hate myself when I do that").

> *The first step I ever took was backwards.*
> —JACKIE VERNON, comedian

The Critical Advisor constricts and corrodes self-confidence, self-approval, self-worth, and self-trust. It becomes a way of thinking, a continual presence that is the increasingly negative lens through which we view ourselves and the challenges we face.

And while those bumps and bruises of life contribute to the Critical Advisor's growth, the real catalyst, the one that invokes and dramatically inflames the Critical Advisor, is the aforementioned Polar Thinking.

Here's how it happens.

A Fertile Breeding Ground

Since Polar Thinking presents only two options, one very desirable and the other very undesirable, the Risk-Reward Guidance System goes awry, into an emergency mode where internal alarms signal fight or flight, "Danger! Danger! Danger!" It's virtually "Do or die!" with no perceived alternatives, no middle ground.

When your mind confronts a situation offering just two possible outcomes, one of which has dire consequences, harmful emotions and attitudes emerge, which poison your perspective and diminish your performance. Those emotions include excessive doubt which eventually leads to fear—fear of failure, fear of embarrassment, and all the other fears you have that short-circuit your potential. They are the toxins released into your consciousness by the Critical Advisor. These are internally created roadblocks to optimum performance.

> *When you beat up on yourself during a match, you've doubled the number of people trying to defeat you.*
> —BRAD GILBERT, America's number-one tennis coach

Polar Thinking's two-option format creates a fertile breeding ground for the emotions of the Critical Advisor. Doubt, anxiety, and fear produce excessive anger, resentment, stress, and a variety of other counterproductive psychological "pains." Negative reinforcement, second-guessing, and increasing amounts of doubt appear. These self-destructive attitudes and emotions are the tools of the Critical Advisor.

When this happens you are pointing the metaphorical pistol right at your performance potential, whether you're on a tennis court or in a sales meeting. Here's what it feels like.

Pointing a Pistol at Your Potential

Perform the following demonstration. Point your index finger out with your thumb skyward as if it were an imaginary gun, like the one you imagined you had as a child playing cowboys. (Please note: actually point your finger out.) Now, point that finger right at your head. Ready? OK, now pull the trigger. Go ahead, feel what it's like. Pull the trigger.

That's exactly what you do when you let your Critical Advisor control your thinking. You shoot down and destroy your performance potential.

Instead of being an affirming presence that believes in your potential (as coach Brad Gilbert helped Andre Agassi do when Agassi went from number 32 to number 1 in the world in twelve months), the Critical Advisor is your own voice of debilitating self-condemnation and negation. Instead of "Just do it," the voice says "Just doubt it"! Bam! The pistol goes off. Self-trust, focus, enjoyment, and relaxation are destroyed and with them your chances for getting in the Zone of high performance.

Critical Advisor Chokes Performance

In sports pressure-induced failure has several names, the *choke*, the *elbow*, or the *collar*. A player can *freeze up*, *break down*, *fall apart*, *lose it*, or *crack*. The terms are interchangeable and simply mean an athlete has failed to perform under pressure. It also happens in business when pressure precludes optimum performance. The pressure is initiated with extreme two-option Polar Thinking.

Choking, or performing at a greatly diminished level, occurs when the Critical Advisor runs amok, when Polar Thinking conjures up a terrible scenario if you should fail and then invites the Critical Advisor to feed you information confirming that you *will* fail. The Critical Advisor whispers in your ear, "You're no good at giving speeches," or "You've never gotten along with [pick the name of a tough client]," or "You always hit the ball in the water here," or "You never buy a stock at the right time!" and much more.

No Choking at the Toaster

Choking doesn't occur when you make toast. Polar Thinking is hard-pressed to construct a win-lose paradigm that is threatening. You understand that the penalty for burning the toast is minimal. Burnt toast? Put another slice in. So what?

However, as the circumstances and stakes change, you perceive that the penalty is more damaging than in the case of your morning slice of toast. You summon up images of increasingly dire results. A big sales presentation, a keynote address, a four-foot putt on the last hole for victory—all are subject to extreme two-option Polar Thinking, which immediately awakens your Critical Advisor. (This also explains why you invariably sink the four-foot putt when it doesn't count, even if you're standing on one foot and holding the putter backward. Since Polar Thinking's win-lose contest mentality is absent for the meaningless putt, so are doubt, anxiousness, and fear. The putt always seems to go in.)

However, at times when something important is at stake, which occurs for successful people on a daily basis, your mind wants to evaluate the Risk-Reward equation with care. It is a normal response but one that becomes almost impossible in the presence of Polar Thinking and the Critical Advisor. In those pressurized circumstances the mind tightens up, or as Gary McCord observed about Greg Norman's mind, it gets "psycho-cramps"; performance suffers.

Your Enemy Within

Remember this: No one can question you as much as your own Critical Advisor. No one can have a lower opinion of you than your Critical Advisor. No one can get in your way as much as your Critical Advisor. And no one can interfere with achieving your optimum performance potential as much as your Critical Advisor.

In short, no one can beat you up the way your Critical Advisor does. It is a virulent presence that transforms you into your own worst enemy. And *you* are the Critical Advisor, your own harshest and most unfair critic!

Super Bowl Winner Stumbles

Three-time Super Bowl winner Randy Cross came to understand this when he joined us for a seminar soon after he retired from a successful career in the NFL.

The San Francisco 49ers have been a preeminent force in professional football for the last fifteen years, during which time they captured four Super Bowl titles. In the mid-1980s one of their premier linemen was 265-pound guard Randy Cross, whose strength, quickness, intelligence, and determination made him All-Pro several times along with teammates Joe Montana, Ronnie Lott, and Jerry Rice.

On the football field Cross knew the attitude associated with unleashing one's greatest potential. "We just understood that we could get the job done. If an assignment was missed, a ball was dropped, or a game was lost we didn't worry about it. It hurt to make a mistake or lose a game, but it never created any doubt about our ability to do it right the next time. We let it go, moved on. At our best we were unconscious." He is, of course, describing the wonderful sense of being in the Zone, of unleashing his optimum performance.

When Cross retired following the 49ers victory over Cincinnati in Super Bowl XXIV, he began a new career, in broadcasting as an analyst with NBC, and found that his previous success and outlook did not transfer immediately to the network's broadcast booth.

Suddenly the former All-Pro came face to face with his own Critical Advisor. "Obviously I made some mistakes on air at first, giving a wrong name or number, a kicked word, sometimes talking over my colleague in the booth—stuff like that. What I found happening was that I began focusing on or worrying about the mistakes. First I worried about them after they happened, and then I found myself worrying about them before they happened. I was getting in my own way."

This is exactly how you think when you let the Critical Advisor take over. You place yourself in a performance straitjacket.

When Cross became aware of this attitudinal change, when he recognized the Critical Advisor as a near-tangible presence, he had taken the first giant step toward exorcising it and hitting his stride as a broadcaster. (Cross recently signed a substantial new network contract.)

What Does Your Critical Advisor Look Like?

Although the Critical Advisor is a mode of thinking and therefore without palpable substance or shape, you will find it extremely helpful to take a moment now to paint a mental picture of what this demon looks like when it appears in your consciousness.

We suggest you picture your own Critical Advisor as a large, grotesque, mosquito-like creature with demoniac red eyes bugging out in a thousand directions and hairy thorns sticking out from its scaly body. It has clawlike feet at the end of bony legs and a black shiny beak that protrudes menacingly. It spews forth a venomous diatribe as it flits around your head drawing your complete attention to itself and its message of doubt, anxiety, fear, and failure.

As you look at it you feel your confidence ebb. It sticks its snout into your neck and sucks out your enthusiasm and faith, your self-trust and enjoyment, and your hope. It leaves you weak.

Please note that you are free to paint this creature in any way you choose. But it is important that you paint the creature in great detail and in a way that conveys the fearful toll this presence extracts, a presence summoned by Polar Thinking. Some have described the creature to us as being similar to the character of the Wicked Witch of the West in the movie *The Wizard of Oz*, a screeching and nagging shrew whose ugliness is exceeded only by her brazen vitriol and harsh criticism.

The face of your Critical Advisor may be an angry bully with bulging eyes and a menacing sneer, shouting and stomping and pounding its fists, demanding that you pay attention to its self-defeating dialogue.

Whatever form you give your Critical Advisor, it is important to see it as a real entity rather than just a pattern of negative thinking. Picturing the form your Critical Advisor takes will facilitate your identifying it when it elbows its way into your consciousness in the future. At the conclusion of this chapter, please take a moment before turning the page to graphically paint a picture in your mind of this loathsome and insidious creature, your Critical Advisor.

For a time we will move away from this opponent within, the Critical Advisor, now that we've discussed what it is, how it emerged, and what it looks like in your mind. We will return to it in Part III, "Your Game Plan," for exorcising Polar Thinking and the Critical Advisor from your consciousness.

At the moment it is only important that you have come to see, like Randy Cross did, the tremendous damage the Critical Advisor does when Polar Thinking allows it to enter and then take over your internal Risk-Reward Guidance System, to control how you think.

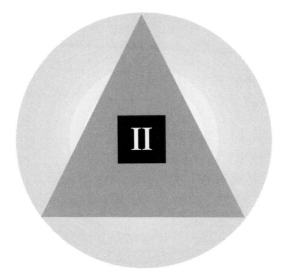

YOUR TEAM

4

THE POWER OF HANDS-FREE

Why Does Montana Smile?

A common view of professional athletes is that they are grown-ups being paid to play children's games. What is often overlooked in this comparison is that to reach their highest level of performance athletes must play those children's games *like children*, specifically, with a spirit of self-trust, awareness, enthusiasm, belief, imagination, and enjoyment. We call this spirit the Power of Hands-Free. When it is present, Polar Thinking and the Critical Advisor are absent. When it is present you are best able to unleash your own full potential.

The Power of Hands-Free personifies the attitudinal and emotional characteristics that are associated with optimum performance (i.e., enjoyment, focused relaxation, and self-trust) and are present when an individual is in the Zone. High achievers like Michael Jordan and Joe Montana and virtually all kids share this special quality and use it to capitalize on and amplify their strengths. You, too, possessed the Power of Hands-Free when you were growing up. Here's an example of it.

"Look, Ma, No Hands!"

At some point as a youngster you wanted to have your own bicycle, and getting that bike became the most important thing in the world. You knew its color (blue). You knew its brand (Schwinn). You knew its size (eighteen-inch wheels). You knew that blue, yellow, and red streamers would be on the grips of its handlebars, or that you'd use clothespins to fasten playing cards against its spokes to make noise. You knew who would get you the bicycle (Mom and Dad). The only thing you didn't know was how to ride a bicycle! Did it matter? Hardly.

You believed that you would get a bicycle, and most wonderful of all was the absolute belief that you would learn how to ride that bicycle. Doubt, anxiety, and fear were absent because of the manner in which you were thinking. That manner of thinking was simply the Power of Hands-Free.

Eventually, of course, you got the bicycle and proceeded to learn how to ride it. In fact, have you ever heard of a youngster who gave up trying to learn how to ride a bicycle? Kids always learn how to ride because they're filled with the Power of Hands-Free.

Hands-Free Riding!

Ultimately the big day arrived when you demonstrated your newfound mastery to your somewhat startled mother. Cruising by on your Schwinn you shouted out in her general direction, "Hey, look, Ma. Look at me!" And when you were sure of her full and undivided attention you threw your arms in the air shouting, "Look, Mom, no hands!" It was a moment of great triumph, riding your bike hands-free, and a valuable example of how to unleash your potential.

In spite of collisions, falls, bumps, bruises, and scratches you had acquired, you learned how to ride that bicycle without ever questioning or doubting yourself. You made the dream happen.

This, of course, is the Power of Hands-Free—the planning, envisioning, and doing with complete self-trust, focus, relaxation, and enjoyment. You had it as a child, and a man nicknamed Joe Cool had it as a quarterback for the San Francisco 49ers.

The Power of (Montana's) Hands-Free

Miami's Dan Marino possessed a more powerful arm, Viking Fran Tarkenton nimbler feet, Pittsburgh's Terry

Bradshaw greater physicality, and Joe Namath of the Super Bowl Jets a more classic release, but former Notre Dame star Joe Montana is generally regarded as the greatest quarterback of the modern era and perhaps the best ever.

What Montana possessed in abundance was the most highly prized commodity in sports, namely, the ability to play big under pressure. He was the guy you wanted in control when the chips were down.

Dan Reeves, most recently coach of the New York Giants and himself a Montana Super Bowl victim in 1990, suggests it's necessary to go to an entirely different sport to find anyone equal to the 49ers' quarterback in this regard. Reeves observes, "As good as they are during the season, it seems they (Larry Bird, Michael Jordan, Magic Johnson, and Montana) raise their level of play the more pressure there is on them during the postseason. They want to play in the big games, and they want the ball in clutch situations." Montana and others do it because they perform with the Power of Hands-Free.

Montana Enjoyed His Job

Green Bay Packers head coach Mike Holmgren served as San Francisco's offensive coordinator during Montana's Super Bowl years. He understands why the legendary quarterback was so effective under pressure. Holmgren says, "I think he [Montana] had a great ability to *have fun* playing and *have fun* practicing and *have fun* going to work" (authors' emphasis). Or, as 49ers head coach Bill Walsh said of his star quarterback, "He played with a smile on his face." Montana enjoyed his work.

Christy Ness, coach of Olympic gold medal figure skater Kristi Yamaguchi, told us the same thing about her famous

Montana had the Power of Hands-Free.

student. "Skating was always a game for Kristi. She always had a sense of play about practice and performance. In fact, during the Olympic performance that won her the gold medal, she missed her triple loop because she was enjoying the music so much, was so engrossed in it, that she forgot it was coming up until it was too late. Skating was just always fun for her."

You'll recall from Chapter 1, "The Paradox of Performance," that this view of one's profession as play is a characteristic common in sports and absent in our own corporate or business environment.

As intensely competitive as Montana (or Yamaguchi) was, he understood that to play football at an optimum level it had to be pleasurable. He actively tried to keep it that way for himself and his teammates. Consciously and intuitively he refused to accept the misguided perspective of Polar Thinking and the self-destructive force of the Critical Advisor. He was able to do this because of his ability to consistently envelop himself in the Power of Hands-Free.

Super Joe at the Super Show

In 1989's Super Bowl XXIII, the 49ers trailed Cincinnati 16–13 with just three minutes and ten seconds remaining when they took possession of the ball on their own eight-yard line. As the team huddled in their end zone to begin a final do-or-die drive, Montana could see discernible tension on the faces of some of his teammates, most noticeably Harris Barton, an outstanding offensive tackle who had a tendency to get uptight.

At the same time Montana glanced up and coincidentally spotted a famous comedian sitting in the stands of Miami's Joe Robbie Stadium. In what he later described as a calculated effort to reduce tension, Montana yelled out, "Hey, isn't that John Candy over there?" Lineman Barton (and others) looked, nodded, and appeared to relax slightly. The brittle and pressurized atmosphere in the 49ers' huddle was broken, and the team settled down. Montana then called the first play in what would be a classic ninety-two-yard effort which culminated in a ten-yard touchdown pass to John Taylor for another Super Bowl victory.

Montana had intentionally and successfully disrupted Barton's and the team's anxiety, doubt, and fear. This discernible tension was the manifestation of focusing on the win-lose nature of the situation (Polar Thinking).

Montana's primary device for keeping his teammates from getting uptight was his own attitude, his ability to utilize the Power of Hands-Free, which is enjoyment, focused relaxation, and self-trust.

The 49ers players looked at their quarterback and saw a man who was comfortable in the situation in spite of the pressure, who was acutely aware but relaxed, and who had total self-confidence. Montana exuded the Power of Hands-Free.

Joy Versus Relief

The following year the 49ers won their fourth Super Bowl, this time against Dan Reeves's Broncos. Unlike Troy Aikman in 1996, Montana again felt joy after the victory, the joy of winning. The game's greatest quarterback understood that preparing, playing, and winning (or losing) was not supposed to be a relief. It was supposed to be fun! And, for Montana, it was fun even in practice. He and other great performers are childlike in this way. They are filled with the Power of Hands-Free.

You will soon bring this same spirit to your work, especially to those situations where the pressure you face is significant.

The Power of Hands-Free is how you went about getting a bicycle and learning how to ride it. The Power of Hands-Free is how Joe Montana approached the challenge of driving ninety-two yards down the field with three minutes and ten seconds remaining in the Super Bowl. It's what he instilled in teammates. The Power of Hands-Free is what produces a smile on Michael Jordan's face at the free throw line. And the Power of Hands-Free is the key to unleashing your greatest potential in your professional endeavors.

Hands-Free Versus the Critical Advisor

The Power of Hands-Free and the Critical Advisor are mutually exclusive modes of thinking that exist within each of us to greater or lesser degrees. The former is self-help while the latter is self-hurt. Identifying both of these presences is necessary because they are continually fighting for space and attention in your consciousness.

THE POWER OF THE PROCESS

It's just you and the ball—Nothin' but ball.
      —ROD LAVER, two-time Grand Slam tennis
      champion

The *present* time is potent because it is where you literally initiate action and affect change. It is where the *process* of performance occurs. This is equally true in sports
or business, whether one is swinging at a baseball in the
World Series or negotiating a contract to manufacture pen-
nants for the World Series.

All great champions will tell you that the secret to optimum performance is the ability to apply one's total concentration to the task at hand—to stay in the Process, the
moment, the now. The Power of Hands-Free occurs in the
present. The Zone occurs only in the present.

Where Is the Process?

Bill Wennington of the Chicago Bulls describes the para-
meters of the Process, the present, as ". . . what's happening now, not what happened two minutes ago, not
what is going to happen in five minutes." His goal? To play
for the "now," where the power is—the power of the
Process.

Tennis legend Chris Evert demonstrated a ferocious ability to play in the present throughout her career. One of
her frequent opponents at the time, Peanut Louie-Harper,
described Evert in the following way: "She was completely
unique on tour in her ability to stay totally in the moment,
totally concentrating on each and every single point
throughout a match regardless of how long it lasted. There
were no ups and downs, no lapses, no mental breaks, no
soft spots when she'd let down. From the first point till
the last point Chris was totally absorbed, not just in each
point but in each stroke within each point. She just gave

you no room to breath at all. There were never any cracks in her concentration."

Evert, winner of eighteen Grand Slam singles titles, acknowledged that her greatest ability was not necessarily in the physical realm but her ability to stay mentally absorbed in the present, the Process. "I've got it here," she said, pointing at her head, indicating where her greatest power existed. By *here* Evert meant her ability to let nothing intrude on the present, the Process.

That is why Polar Thinking and the Critical Advisor are so destructive to your performance potential. They stealthily move into the Process and kick your focus into the future or back to the past. Evert was one of the best ever at avoiding this.

Return to the Future

When you are booted into the future by Polar Thinking, its two-option success-failure scenario becomes the focus of your attention. As we observed in Chapter 3, the Critical Advisor then offers up doubt, anxiety, and fear, a "catastrophizing" way of thinking in which you envision terrible events somewhere on the near or far horizon.

When your attention revisits the past, your Critical Advisor will summon up previous failures, losses, or embarrassments. This, in turn, produces guilt, anger, or sadness—raw materials used by your Critical Advisor to manufacture toxic doses of self-criticism.

The Critical Advisor diverts your mind from the present Process of just doing it to memories of past defeats and setbacks. (For example: "I gave a miserable presentation here last year and lost a big account. The whole quarter was down the drain after that. I hate this kind of forum. It just isn't my best situation.") Self-criticism is heaped on

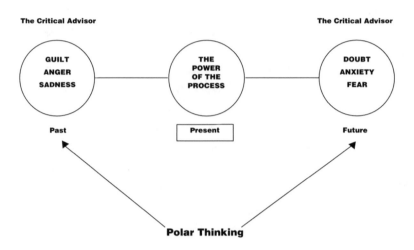

The Power of Hands-Free

self-criticism. Self-trust is mugged and replaced by self-doubt.

Regardless of the direction, past or future, that Polar Thinking and the Critical Advisor takes you, the result is the same. Your participation in and focus on the Process of what you are doing is damaged or destroyed, and along with it goes your performance potential.

You Drive Your Car in the Present

The reason you drive so well is that you are fully absorbed in the Process, in the present, plugged into the task at hand. You drive with the Power of Hands-Free. In fact, you know from your own experience that the worst drivers, the ones who pose the biggest threat, are those who are overly fearful, whose habitual Polar Thinking and Critical Advisor have reduced them to looking both ways ten times before driving through an intersection at a crawl. They have been virtually paralyzed by a thought process that replaces the Power of Hands-Free with Polar Thinking and the Critical Advisor.

It happens in cars, and it happens in corporations. You can probably think of someone currently in your organization who is always hesitant to act, to *do*. It is because he or she is preoccupied with Polar Thinking and his or her Critical Advisor. This person becomes immobilized like the fearful driver who looks back and forth ten times at an intersection.

Kristi Yamaguchi Postpones Her Wheaties

Kristi Yamaguchi's coach, Christy Ness, understood the importance of staying in the Process when her student won the World Championship in Munich in 1991. Ness explained her thinking to us recently at the Oakland–U.S. Ice Center in Oakland, California. "We decided not to get an agent for Kristi after she won the World Championship even though the endorsement potential was great. I believe she never would have gotten the Olympic gold medal ten months later if she had acquired an agent. It would have thrown her focus off the daily process."

Why? Because the endorsement money would have been tied to Yamaguchi's *future* Olympic results. Her coach and others realized there was enough pressure built into the competition without adding a million-dollar payoff to the mix. They knew how easy it would be for their skater to shift attention from the Process of preparation to the huge financial payoff and the consequences of a poor performance (two-option Polar Thinking).

It was for this same reason that Coach John Wooden scrupulously avoided using the words *win* or *winning* during the basketball season. He intuitively understood that it would shift players' focus off the Process of preparation to the consequence of the contest.

UCLA coach John Wooden says winning was never mentioned.

As the legendary coach explained during our conversations, "I never mentioned the word *winning* because it took concentration off what we were working on at the moment, disrupted the preparation."* Wooden understood the importance of keeping his team's attention focused in the present and off the perceived rewards or threats of the upcoming game.

---

*Coach Wooden went even further in his efforts in this regard. After a victory he refused to say that UCLA "beat" the other team. Instead he referred to the results by saying UCLA had "outscored" the opponent as he constantly attempted to stress the Process over the prize. "Beat" suggests the win-lose format of Polar Thinking. "Outscored" is much less suggestive of a contest mentality. His philosophy is detailed further in *Wooden: A Lifetime of Observations and Reflections On and Off the Court* (Wooden and Jamison, Contemporary Books, 1997).

Turn Out the Lights

When your focus is moved from the Process to the past or future during performance, you can "turn out the lights; the party's over," as Don Meredith used to croon on ABC's *Monday Night Football*. The party could have been over in Super Bowl XXIII for Harris Barton of the 49ers, except that Joe Montana yanked his focus back to the present and away from the anxiety created by Polar Thinking and the Critical Advisor.

For the same reason, the party was almost over for future senator Bill Bradley after his first year as a pro in the NBA. Outside influences had reached into his consciousness and redirected his focus, allowing Polar Thinking and the Critical Advisor to move him away from the Process.

Bill Bradley: Outside Expectations

Princeton's (future senator) Bill Bradley was one of the most remarkable basketball players in collegiate history. In 1965 he led his unranked Tigers to Portland, Oregon, and the March Madness of the NCAA's Final Four, which included Cazzie Russell's Michigan Wolverines, Wichita State, and John Wooden's UCLA Bruins with Lew Alcindor (later known as Kareem Abdul-Jabbar).

During the tournament (eventually won by Wooden's Bruins) Bradley set individual game play-off records for scoring, fifty-eight points, and field goals, twenty-two shots made from the floor, records previously held by Oscar Robertson.

Additionally, Bradley's 177 points set a new tournament record, and he was subsequently voted most valuable player in the national championships. He was an All-American who was also a Rhodes scholar.

Then suddenly Bradley retired from the game. He chose to continue his education at Oxford University in England and rejected a very lucrative offer from the New York Knicks to play pro ball. Bradley intended to get on with a life away from basketball.

But in 1967 he reversed direction and joined the Knicks as one of the highest-paid rookies in the history of the game. His perceived abilities and value had increased during his absence from the game.

The press dubbed him Dollar Bill, and the public eagerly awaited the immediate miracles he would perform in a Knicks uniform. However, for the first time in his life Bradley began struggling on the court. Expectations were too high and the competition much different than in college. Bradley had been in academia for two years and would need time to adjust to the level of performance he saw in teammates Walt Frazier, Dave DeBusschere, Willis Reed, and others around the league.

Bradley floundered and soon felt the increasing sting of the press and public's criticism as they rushed to declare him a failure. Dollar Bill was devalued and subjected to verbal attacks on the street, in cabs, and as he walked in and out of Madison Square Garden. The Rhodes scholar was unaccustomed to being called a "no-good worthless bum" when he left an arena after a game, but it became the norm. The streets of New York City were considerably less civil than the lanes of Oxford.

Bradley was averaging just eight points per game, and the public's hash rejection affected his attitude, confidence, and ultimately his performance as the season wore on. His attention was shifting from the immediate and enormous requirements of the Process of playing NBA basketball to the results and all that was being written and said about him publicly. The season became torturous.

Bradley's ultimate reaction and performance demonstrates the enormous importance of staying in the present, in the Process. He decided that the public rejection of his output on the basketball court allowed him to reject the public and its expectations. Bradley resolved to play solely for himself, his team, and the game without concern for the public's evaluation and opinion of his work. He returned to a steely focus on just the game, the Process.

He ceased worrying about what people might say in the future or had written about him in the past. Bradley used this painful public disapproval to grant himself what was his all along, namely, the right to play for himself in the moment, to focus on just the Process.

By the start of his second year, he had consciously shifted his focus away from public expectancies and opinions to a more immediate issue. "I came to feel that it was my performance on the court and the integrity of what we were doing there in and of itself that matters and that the millions watching were incidental to what the craft was. And that realization was liberating." Bradley had shifted his attention and focus from future results back to the power of the Process. He had removed Polar Thinking and the Critical Advisor from his consciousness, but only after they had made his first year as a professional miserable.

Bradley had courageously decided to just do it instead of worrying about whether in the public eye he could just do it right. He was subsequently able to unleash his greatest efforts on the court.

In the nine seasons that followed, Bradley helped his team win two NBA championships (1970 and 1973) and regained his position as one of basketball's most respected competitors. Bradley had gotten back into the Process.

Staying in the Moment Is Magic

Two-time Grand Slam tennis champion Rod Laver describes this state of concentration, this staying in the Process, as seeing "nothing but ball." During a match, Laver often became totally oblivious to the opponent, the wind, the sun, the noise, the crowd, and any ultimate gain or loss attached to the competition. During a game he saw (and thought about) only the tennis ball, which began to look "as big as a grapefruit." He stayed totally in the Process and brought forth his best efforts by blocking out the distractions of Polar Thinking and the Critical Advisor.

Pressure Can Lower Your IQ

Brad Gilbert, tennis coach of Andre Agassi, described in his colorful way what can happen when you succumb to Polar Thinking. He said, "Pressure can make a person stupid! You do stupid things because your mind starts thinking about the wrong stuff." Gilbert, recently voted America's number-one coach, knew that anxiety and tension (brought on by Polar Thinking) are crippling forces that can dramatically alter mental and physical behavior.

A current tennis champion, Pete Sampras, had the good fortune to be taught by individuals who understood the importance of staying in the present and focusing on the Process without peeking at the prize, the result. "When I was a kid my parents and coaches were more concerned about my playing well than about winning," Sampras recalled. That philosophy is espoused today by his current coach, Paul Annacone, who described a simple view of a serious issue. He said, "Pressure is what you make it out to be. You can't be thinking about winning or losing before or during a match, or it's all over before it's even started."

It's all over because focusing on the winning-losing (Polar Thinking) allows the Critical Advisor to start playing its own game with your mind. It can make you "stupid."

The result for Sampras is that he currently demonstrates such complete poise under pressure that at times it appears he is on the verge of falling asleep (or is he simply in the Zone?). As much by training as by temperament he has a ferocious ability to stay in the Process.

Understand that champions like Sampras, Jordan, Laver, Bradley, Montana, and others comprehend the profound rewards and consequences inherent in competition at their level of play. In addition to seeking the benefits of fame and fortune, they are natural competitors of the highest order.

What makes them unique is their ability to keep their eyes *off* the prize, the result, and on the Process of performance. This ability to stay in the Process is what separates them from the pack.

Bill Walsh's Standard of Performance

Here's how three-time Super Bowl winner, coach Bill Walsh, described to us his approach to keeping his team in the Process. "We thought very little about the prize. It was just continually how we performed, how we were going to improve, how we were going to enhance our skills. We related to our own standard of performance, trying to achieve that rather than relating to a given opponent. Let the opponents take care of themselves. We were able to channel the concentration of the team toward performance with as little force from outside influences [e.g., Bill Bradley's distraction with media and public expectations] as possible."

Coach Walsh immersed himself and the team in the Process of preparation. "It was a block-by-block building of a standard of performance in which our performance level was hopefully higher than that of our opponents. That's where our concern was. By focusing strictly on our own standard of performance, we were able to play the bigger games very very well, because it was basically business as usual. The point is that the standard of performance is what counts. The score takes care of itself."

This ability to ferociously control focus, to concentrate solely on the Process to the virtual exclusion of concern for result (e.g., Walsh's preoccupation with building a standard of performance), is difficult in normal circumstances. It becomes almost impossible when you are unwittingly dragged out of the present and into the future (or past) by Polar Thinking and the Critical Advisor. And to stay firmly entrenched in the present, you must have a powerful Game Plan (Part III).

There is an additional significant advantage to staying in the Process.

What You Focus on Expands

You may recall an interesting phenomenon that occurred last time you purchased a new car. Once you made the decision to buy the automobile, you immediately became aware of how many other buyers had purchased the exact same car (and in the same color!) you had. Whereas you may have noticed a few on the road previously, it now seemed as if your new automobile was the car of choice.

This is because what you focus on expands. If you buy a new set of Ping golf clubs you'll suddenly become aware of all those other golfers who also have the same clubs, even the same color-coded grips. Buy a new Rolex and suddenly you'll notice how many people have that same watch.

The reason for this is very logical. You seek corresponding evidence supporting whatever you have chosen to invest time, money, or effort in. When your first child arrived, suddenly everyone you talked with had a brand-new baby. "And what kind of diapers do you think are best?" you asked them.

Was it coincidence? No. It happens because what you focus on (a purchase or a new baby) expands. It is a normal reaction and one that has enormous potential for helping or hurting you in the following way.

When you are focused on the Process of performance, of *doing*, your mind will effortlessly and automatically begin to seek out supporting evidence and information to help you accomplish the task at hand.

Conversely, when your focus has been broken and shifted, when you are taken out of the present by the force of Polar Thinking and the Critical Advisor, your mind will seek to support whatever negative perspective they bring forth. In effect, you will attempt to give validation to the counterproductive scenario produced by your Critical Advisor.

Concentrate on the Process and your mind will help you accomplish it. Let Polar Thinking and your Critical Advisor shift attention forward or backward (to prior failures or future consequences) and your mind will seek out corresponding and supporting evidence for it.

So the old maxim, Think you can, and think you can't—either way you'll be right, has great truth because what you focus on expands.

Think you can make the sale to an important client (the Power of Hands-Free) and your mind will find corresponding evidence to reinforce what you are focusing on and trying to achieve. If you think a big client will say no (the Critical Advisor), your mind will quickly provide evidence that you are correct.

> *I only care about one thing, the present.*
> —JIMMY JOHNSON, coach of the Miami
> Dolphins

The great achievers in every walk of life, most visibly in sports, have the ability to immerse themselves in the Process, which subsequently directs their minds toward accomplishing the goals. They have the mental muscle (and it requires tremendous strength) to keep their focus in the present to the exclusion of future results. It is a fundamental difference between consistently high achievers and everyone else.

Bill Bradley the basketball star was able to return to the present with his circuitous rationale and analysis. Joe Montana has always had an innate ability to focus on the process. Both arrived at the same place mentally and had great careers. Evert, Yamaguchi and other high achievers share the same ability.

The Game Plan, detailed in Part III, will give you the mental technology to do the same in your professional endeavors, to have access to and apply a mental technology that will keep you in the Process, where the power is.

The Leverage of
Language

An Overlooked Impact Player

You are familiar with the concept of *leverage* as applied to financial matters. Simply put, it means that a smaller object properly used has the power to move (or acquire) a larger object. A down payment of $50,000 may give you the leverage to purchase a home valued at $500,000 (if you're lucky).

The concept of leverage applies to language as well. Words are small objects that when properly utilized have the power to have an enormous impact on larger objects. One of those larger objects is you and your performance potential.

A Brief Word About Words

Many words are neutral and act simply as transporters of more potent words. Pronouns, conjunctions, and prepositions such as *this, that, but, for, of,* and *and* are examples. However, most words evoke increasingly automatic responses of varying kind and degree in us. Depending on their combinations and context those responses can be minor or major. More important, as it relates to your performance potential, those responses can be extremely productive or counterproductive, positive or negative.

The advertising industry exploits your automatic response to words and the images and emotions they evoke by carefully selecting and crafting them so as to get you to do certain things, to leverage you into the action of buying their product. They know if the words are chosen and utilized correctly you will respond in a predictable and unconscious manner. They understand the power words have on you.

What's So Great About Shredded Wheat?

A good example is that box of cereal on your breakfast table. Study it instead of the newspaper the next time you have coffee on Sunday morning. Notice the words and phrases judiciously selected to appear on a box of Nabisco Shredded Wheat include *wholesome, pure, lightly toasted, 100 percent natural, crunchy biscuit, high quality, original, family, fresh, whole wheat,* and *great taste.* Those words are chosen with care.

Each has been weighed, analyzed, and measured as to its individual and collective impact on you. Every single word is evocative. In fact, reading the list out of context should make you hungry for Shredded Wheat, which is exactly why they were chosen.

Your brain produces predictable mental images (you think, "Pure, lightly toasted crunchy biscuits of delicious whole wheat? Yum, yum!") as a result of being exposed to those words. Advertisers and marketers realistically expect that you will do certain things as a result, namely, buy and eat Nabisco Shredded Wheat.

You'll notice words and phrases such as *dry, tastes like hay, flavorless,* and *expensive* are rarely printed on the side of a box of cereal, for the same reason. Those words are also very evocative, but experts know they will automatically push you away from their product.

Advertisers are keenly aware of the inherent power of words and try to exploit them in order to do one of the most difficult things in the entire world, namely, get you to voluntarily take money out of your pocket and turn it over to them. That is big leverage as created by little words.

Crafting Your Own Vocabulary

The words you choose in your own internal and external dialogue (i.e., those you intentionally and unintentionally say and think) are as potent as those the marketing experts judiciously select to appear on your box of cereal. The primary difference is that Nabisco chooses words with an acute understanding of the impact they will have. They place the words carefully on the box of cereal like a verbal minefield ready to detonate images, emotions, and actions when your eyes "step" on them. They understand the Leverage of Language.

Your own word selection, the collection of words chosen by you rather than a cereal maker, is habitual, unpremeditated, and done without keen knowledge of the words' impact on you and others. The next few pages will radically alter this. (Note: we specifically chose the word *radically* to leverage your interest, to denote that the upcoming ideas will be significant and transformational. Ours was a premeditated word choice decision to use the Leverage of Language on you.)

The Language of Inclusion (or Exclusion)

Ask a child who has just visited Disneyland with his parents how it was, and the response will be, "It was great!" Ask the parent who has just enjoyed the same experience for a reaction and the answer may be, "It was not bad at all. It wasn't as crowded as I expected, and the prices weren't too steep—really not a bad deal at all."

Notice the difference in what is described. The child tells you what *is* while the adult tells you what *isn't*. (Child: "It *is* great." Adult: "It *isn't* bad, *isn't* crowded, *isn't* expensive, *isn't* a bad deal.")

One (the child's) is the Language of Inclusion, while the other (the parent's) is the Language of Exclusion. Both are extremely powerful; the former in a productive way because it is the dynamic language of the Power of Hands-Free, the latter in a constraining way because it operates in the vernacular of the Critical Advisor.

Unfortunately over the years most adults become habitual users of the Language of Exclusion, the vocabulary of doubt, absence, omission, equivocation, and diminution. It is a language of hesitancy, anxiety, and fear and will tell you what isn't, couldn't, shouldn't, can't, and won't (please recall Chapter 3, "The Critical Advisor").

It is the vocabulary of "don't" and is common among politicans who describe to us what an opponent can't do ("He can't get legislation passed") or what they themselves are not. Notice the difference in your perception if instead of announcing, "I am not a crook," Richard M. Nixon had said, "I am an innocent man." The former is exclusionary. The latter is inclusionary. One evokes darkness, the other one light.

The former is also the language we use on ourselves with great damage. "Hey, that isn't a bad idea!" Do you mean it is a good idea? "I can't complain about my health." Do you mean you are healthy? "Nobody gives you a better deal than we do." Do you mean that you offer the best deal? "I can't remember when I've enjoyed a meal this much." Do you mean this is the finest meal you can remember? Each exclusionary response is limiting and cautionary. They are the responses of the driver who looks both ways ten times before proceeding.

Does It Matter?

At this point are you wondering if concern for language and choice of words is an important matter, that regardless of how you say things everybody knows what you mean.

Speaking in the Language of Exclusion, that is, speaking of absence and of what is not, takes its toll on our attitudes and subsequent performance. Exclusionary language is cautionary rather than compelling, self-limiting rather than expansive and emboldening. It is timid, circuitous, and avoidance directed. It moves our focus, our concentration, away from what we want to do to what we *don't* want to do, from what is to what isn't.

This use (or misuse) of words is pervasive in our culture. A staff member recently said, "Not a day goes by that I don't want to come to work!" We took it as a positive statement and asked her how the same sentiment could be expressed using the Language of Inclusion. She thought for a moment and said, "I really look forward to coming to work each day!" The same idea was expressed in two different languages. The Language of Inclusion expressed it in a productive, contagious, and positive way. I liked hearing it. She felt better saying it.

Coach Bill Walsh described to us his appreciation for the power of words. He said, "You demonstrate a lack of assuredness when you start talking negatives. In coaching you always take a supportive approach rather than a negative approach." Walsh understands what an impact player language can be.

The Language of Inclusion is powerful because it directs our thoughts and actions toward specific productive actions. Sales quotas work because they direct us toward a target rather than away from something. They are inclusionary, the language of "do" rather than "don't."

Which is more likely to get results, "Let's give it everything we've got and go over the top on this month's sales quota!" or "Let's really give it everything we've got so we don't fall short."? Obviously, the Language of Inclusion is more dynamic and compelling.

The Language of Inclusion is an accelerator when it comes to performance potential. The Language of Exclusion puts the brakes on your performance.

Positive Actions Begin with Positive Words

Words create images. Images create emotions. Emotions dramatically affect perceptions and performance. It's true for a box of cereal, and it's exponentially true as it applies to you. The Language of Inclusion utilizes a supportive, directed, positive, and trusting vocabulary that sets a course of action (achievement) and sustains you along the way. It keeps you in the present, in the Process of doing.

Nike's Language of Inclusion

Because positive actions begin with positive words is why Nike's "Just do it" slogan is arguably the most compelling advertising phrase to come forth in half a century. It is the ultimate Power of Hands-Free language and gave millions of sedentary individuals with strong Critical Advisors the freedom to begin active lifestyles instead of second-guessing, questioning, fearing, or doubting themselves.

The positive exhortation "Just do it" removed couch potatoes' Critical Advisors in the boldest possible way. The phrase inspired people to bypass concern about whether they could do it, whether someone else might do it better, whether they would lose if they did it, whether they might be embarrassed while doing it, and a variety of other doubts and fears. It was the epitome of inclusionary language.

In essence the slogan gave millions of people the license to forget about their Critical Advisors and "just do it!" It was a transforming and liberating phrase and a great example of the force inherent in the Language of Inclusion.

Those three words are so powerful that billions of dollars worth of running shoes and athletic gear have been sold in large part because of their dynamic inclusionary force.

The opposite is true for corporate couch potatoes who are constrained by the hesitant and limiting Language of Exclusion. They say "I don't have a problem with that," rather than "I think you have a good idea!" Which would you rather hear after making a presentation? Which would be more apt to create positive energy in your business environment? Yes, words have a profound impact on our attitude and resulting behavior. The late Harvey Penick, author of the best-selling *Little Red Book* and a master golf instructor, understood this. He wrote, "I try to put everything in positive, constructive terms." He recognized the power of using inclusionary language that directed his students in terms of what *should* be done rather than what *should not* be done. He amusingly described his philosophy in an exclusionary style, "When I am teaching I never say *never* and I don't say *don't*." It was humorous but astute.

Exclusionary and Inclusionary Thinking

The manner in which we use language influences our perspective in life. The amateur golfer who stands on the tee telling himself where he doesn't want to hit the ball ("Don't hit it in the water") is using exclusionary language, which invokes the dire consequences that accompany two-option Polar Thinking. By telling himself what he doesn't want to do he automatically and subconsciously thinks about why he doesn't want to do it and what will happen if he fails.

In addition to inducing anxiety with this avoidance dialogue, the golfer has neglected to give himself a specific plan for what he *does* want to do.

A PGA touring pro performs with tremendously directed and inclusionary language and thinking. When Jack Nicklaus stands over a ball, his mind is seeing the target—where he wants the ball to go rather than where he doesn't want it to land. The hacker thinks "Don't go in the water"; the Golden Bear thinks "Go in the hole."

Inclusionary language is the language of performance, the language of achievement, the language of the Process. It is the language of the Power of Hands-Free.

Martin Mazzanti, owner of the Produce Exchange in San Francisco, a company with annual revenues of more than $65 million, has come to realize the force of language in the corporate environment. Mazzanti's entire sales staff has worked conscientiously on learning and incorporating the Language of Inclusion into their professional lives, using it rather than its negative counterpart. Results? Mazzanti says, "Now my people are always thinking in terms of what we will do, what we want to accomplish. A mistake or failure is seen only as an opportunity to learn. [The Language of Inclusion] has made a huge difference in our company. We've learned to speak a common language, the language of high performance."

High-Performance Words

As we noted, the key to performance is to remain focused on the process of doing, to stay in the hands-free moment and away from Polar Thinking and the Critical Advisor.

One of the primary tools that allows you to accomplish this is language—word power.

A Challenge

This book is meant to be accessible and educational—easily read, absorbed, and applied in an immediately useful manner. However, there are two elements of *In the Zone* that are going to require great discipline and effort to incorporate into your life. The most challenging one is addressed in Chapter 13, "Notice (The Awareness Question)." The other challenge is what we have described here, namely, learning to use the Language of Inclusion while simultaneously eliminating the Language of Exclusion. It will require that you break a habit that's been in place for decades. However, you can do it!

Begin by observing how others express themselves. Be alert to their use of exclusionary words and phrases, *shouldn't, couldn't, can't, won't,* and others listed at the end of this chapter. You'll be amazed at how frequently people speak in terms of what isn't there, what they aren't, what won't happen, and more (or less). It is the terminology of omission rather than of commission.

Pay careful attention to your own word selection. Monitor your use of language. Accentuate what is there, namely, what's present, the positive, the Language of Inclusion. Give your vocabulary the same attention that marketing experts bestow on the copy on a box of cereal.

To help you do this we've compiled a list of examples of exclusionary language that are commonly used. Also listed is the inclusionary language you can employ as you remove the language of exclusion from your vocabulary.

The Language of Exclusion	The Language of Inclusion
"I can't complain."	"I feel good!"
"I can't argue with that."	"I tend to agree with that."
"I couldn't ask for more."	"I'm very pleased."
"I don't disagree."	"I agree."
"If you don't, then we won't."	"If you do, then we will."
"I don't expect anything less."	"Here's what I expect . . ."
"I hope I don't choke."	"I hope I do well."
"I don't see why not."	"Let's do it."
"I won't stand in your way."	"I'll stay out of your way."
"If nothing gets in our way . . ."	"If everything goes as planned . . ."
"Don't get upset!"	"Relax."
"Don't hit the ball in the water."	"Hit the ball on the green."
"No problem."	"It's a pleasure."
"That's not bad."	"That's good."
"It's not as bad as it seems."	"It's better than it seems."
"Why don't we . . ."	"Let's . . ."
"That's not a bad idea."	"That's a good idea."

The Language of Exclusion	The Language of Inclusion
"That's not what I'm saying."	"Here's what I'm saying."
"Why wouldn't we want to . . ."	"Let's consider."

As you noticed, the Language of Inclusion moves ideas and actions forward. It creates momentum and force and is a fundamental element of the Power of Hands-Free. Starting now, here, in the present, use this great power to your own advantage instead of having it used against you by yourself and others. Then you'll begin to feel like you do when the sun comes out on a dreary day—enthusiastic, positive, confident, and self-assured.

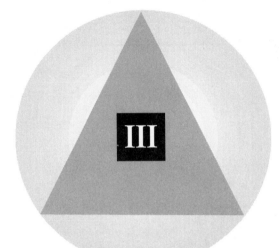

YOUR GAME PLAN

The Perry Principles

THE MENTAL
MANAGEMENT
STYLE OF WINNERS

Consistent and superior performers in every walk of life have a formidable ability to turn almost any situation to their psychological and practical advantage. They expect to do well, and when it happens they embrace their success and use the results to help them achieve even greater productivity, in effect, capitalizing on their strengths. They are skilled at staying in the Process with the Power of Hands-Free (and this is what *In the Zone* will enable you to accomplish).

Conversely, when conditions exist that bring forth Polar Thinking and the Critical Advisor, superior performers have an ability to recover quickly, controlling negative emotions or attitudes, and to return quickly to the Power of Hands-Free. They exhibit a continuum of positive perspective, a focus on the immediate effort (i.e., they're task oriented), and a resiliency of attitude and spirit that precludes any significant or long-term self-bashing.

The Perry Principles, in Part III, "Your Game Plan," will provide you with the tools to do the same, to unleash your greatest performance potential by capitalizing on your strengths and recovering quickly from setbacks and weaknesses. It is a mental technology for staying in the Process of performance and achieving optimum results, for getting you near or into the Zone.

How Losers Lose

Those who consistently perform at suboptimum levels have a different mental technology. They constantly knock themselves out of the Process of performance with Polar Thinking's two-option win-lose format and the Critical Advisor's incessant self-bashings. Furthermore, they often embrace the negative results ("This always seems to happen to me" or "I can't win for losing") while being suspicious of the positive ("It must be some kind of mistake" and "This won't last").

When this happens, the stage is set for diminished performance results and reduced enjoyment. Such people are miserable regardless of whether they succeed or fail.

Keep Your Eye *Off* the Prize

One of the most important ideas we can convey to you is that while winning is wonderful—it's why we keep score in sports and life—allowing it to continuously occupy a central position in your mind's eye is the wrong Game Plan. It is a formula for inducing Polar Thinking and the Critical Advisor. Focusing on "I've got to win" means you'll also be focusing on "What happens if I lose?" While all of this is going on in your mind, your performance potential is dropping precipitously. It is what Coach Brad Gilbert referred to with his observation "Pressure makes you stupid."

Top achievers, the ones who in addition to succeeding also enjoy the experience, focus on Process to the exclusion of prize (see Chapter 5). They are able to take their enormous appetite for success, achievement, fame, winning, or victory and compartmentalize it. They put it away while the Process unfolds. Letting the Process unfold is what Rod Laver means when he describes seeing "nothing but ball."

The following chapters will detail for you exactly how to see nothing but ball in your own professional and personal endeavors.

"In the Zone" Equals "In the Process"

Dick Gould, men's tennis coach at Stanford University and NCAA Division I Coach of the Decade for the 1980s (and recently voted Coach of the Year) understands how important being in the Zone can be. Gould's record is one of the most spectacular in the history of college tennis and was enhanced in 1996 when his team captured its fourteenth NCAA championship in men's tennis.

The view he shared with us is direct. He said, "I probably hurt us [Stanford men's tennis] earlier in my career by overstressing winning national championships and my great desire for that to happen. The team felt the pressure, and it affected them adversely." Essentially he was directing his team's attention to the prize to the exclusion of the Process.

Gould began to understand that the team had to shift its focus off the prize and onto the Process to maximize abilities and results. He subsequently changed his message. "I let them [the players] know I was measuring their success in terms of day-to-day improvement. My players knew that improvement was my criterion. If you made improvement, you knew you were succeeding."

The Stanford coach explained the importance of the Process when he said "You have to be champion of your block before you're champion of the city. Learning, improvement, is success."

Gould understood that letting his team believe the season would be a failure if they produced anything less than a national championship added enormous and counterproductive pressure. This pressure made it even more difficult to achieve victory. Focusing on the prize pulled his team out of the present.

Gould got his team into the present so they could win in the future. That's when Stanford's national titles in tennis started accumulating.

When Winning Is Everything

As we've seen, Greg Norman, Boris Becker, Troy Aikman, and even Michael Jordan damaged themselves in varying ways at different times because they allowed Polar Thinking, winning or losing, to take over their consciousness at the expense of Process. And, of course, there are thousands of athletes you've never heard of who were eliminated because Polar Thinking destroyed them before they ever appeared in the sports pages. The same is true in the less public but equally volatile environment of business.

Before we draw up your Game Plan for unleashing top performance efforts, for staying in the Process, let's briefly check what we've seen earlier in Part I, "The Opponent," and Part II, "Your Team."

Instant Replay: In the Zone

We know that optimum performance, the Zone, occurs most often when you are enjoying the experience—focused, aware, relaxed, and self-confident—and when the Power of Hands-Free is in abundance and the Language of Inclusion is the vocabulary of choice.

However, we are taught to believe work is inherently unpleasant, stressful, and joyless and produces self-doubt. How can it be work if it's fun? In fact we have been conditioned to understand that this "pain," the unpleasantness, actually adds value. Thus, many executives wear their pain like a badge of honor.

And since we are conditioned to accept this pain as necessary in the context of work, we use it as a standard for determining how hard we are working and how productive we are being. Unfortunately, most of us have difficulty distinguishing when we are working hard in the most productive manner from when we have crossed over to a level of stress, anxiety, and ill-temper that is extremely counterproductive. We think more pain means more gain, even though we know in our gut it diminishes performance, enjoyment, and the subsequent results for ourselves and those we work with.

Polar Thinking and the Critical Advisor

Furthermore, our scorecard mentality positions most situations in a pain-producing, win-lose paradigm called Polar Thinking. This habitual two-option, results-oriented mode forces us to confront the likelihood of dire consequences, which in turn sets off the Critical Advisor. This is the dark and marauding presence that knocks us off balance and out of the present, out of the Process, by creating doubt. This gives way to anxiety and fear, ultimately, even to choking. As we know, these are fundamental roadblocks to optimum performance results.

The Language of Exclusion

We nourish our Critical Advisor with the Language of Exclusion which shouts "can't," "won't," "couldn't," "shouldn't," and "don't" in our ears. It is skeptical, whining, doubting, cynical, questioning, untrusting, and "catastrophizing." It is a psychological and emotional barrier to initiative, effectiveness, and enjoyment. It limits your tremendous potential. And, yet we interpret this self-torment, this pain, as being normal and productive in the context of work.

The Power of Hands-Free

All of this is done at the expense of the Power of Hands-Free, that natural and powerful spirit we have within us at birth that is slowly squeezed out as we mature. The Power of Hands-Free is the essence of optimum potential and performance. Kids manifest it when they learn to ride a bicycle with their hands off the handlebars, as do most superior athletes when they prepare for, meet, and respond to challenges and goals. It is the empowering spirit that supports, trusts, and speaks in the Language of Inclusion, the positive and directed language of "do" that tells us "I can and will."

The Perry Principles: Surge-Recover-Surge

Obviously then the key to unleashing your fullest potential is to be able to ignite the Power of Hands-Free while also knowing how to recover quickly from conditions that produce Polar Thinking and the Critical Advisor.

This performance methodology is called Surge-Recover-Surge. We'll repeat it again, because when you incorporate it into your life you will have the Game Plan for staying in the Process and achieving optimum performance. Surge-Recover-Surge!

Simply put, it means you will Surge on the Power of Hands-Free, quickly Recover when setbacks or doubt awaken your Critical Advisor and take you out of the Process, and then return immediately to the Process of surging on the Power of Hands-Free. Surge-Recover-Surge—it is the key to consistent high achievement and consistent enjoyment along the way.

Surge (on the Power of Hands-Free) means focus, awareness, and self-trust before, during, and after performance tasks. It means capitalizing on your strengths, successes, good thoughts and feelings, and belief in yourself.

Recover (from the Critical Advisor) means quickly removing the doubt, anxiety, and lowered self-trust you often inflict on yourself. It is recovering promptly from your setbacks and weaknesses. Surge-Recover-Surge!

Ironically, most adults spend their lives doing the opposite. They allow their Critical Advisors to surge, which highlights and amplifies their weaknesses—doubt, anxiety, and fear. At the same time they inhibit the Power of Hands-Free by questioning the value of enjoyment, the legitimacy of self-confidence, and the appropriateness of focused relaxation.

They handcuff themselves by capitalizing on their weaknesses instead of their strengths. This is about to change for you. The next four chapters will provide you with a step-by-step Game Plan, a formula or recipe that will allow you to consistently surge on the Power of Hands-Free:

Surge: RVOC

Ritualize (Sharpen Your Focus)
Visualize (Preview Your Performance)
Optimize (Turn It Up and Just Do It)
Capitalize (Celebrate Your Success)

Following this, we will present the equally important Game Plan to recover quickly from the destructive impact of conditions that create Polar Thinking and your Critical Advisor:

Recover: NOLD

Notice (The Awareness Question)
Options-Learning (The Empowerment Question)
Do Differently (The Recovery Question)

This is your Game Plan for unleashing your greatest potential, RVOC plus NOLD. It is a formula you will successfully apply in future performance situations, in preparing for them, executing them, and reacting to subsequent results. Whether it's making a corporate sales presentation, presenting a speech at your industry's annual convention, negotiating with your boss for a promotion, responding to a setback, or preparing for challenges of every type, you'll Surge-Recover-Surge and prosper with self-confidence, enjoyment, and success.

Welcome Critical Carl from Cleveland

Before proceeding, we would like to introduce you to someone who will join us for the rest of our journey in *In the Zone*. His name is Critical Carl from Cleveland. Critical Carl has spent fifteen years successfully selling life insurance and has provided his family (wife, Ruth, and nine-year-old son, Mason) with a very comfortable lifestyle.

Recently, however, Critical Carl from Cleveland has struggled to achieve the performance levels he obtained in earlier years. Whether it's the economy, the competition, or something he's unintentionally changed in his selling style, top performance results are much tougher to come by. Coincidentally, or because of it, he has also lost his zest for the challenge. His job has increasingly become a joyless struggle.

"Critical Carl, is this a reasonable description of what's going on?" we asked.

"Absolutely," he replied. "Whatever is causing it, I'm off my game and have been increasingly over the last few years. I used to look forward to the tough sale. I guess it brought out my competitive instincts—not any more. It's become a struggle, and I could use some direction."

"Critical Carl," we promised, "you are about to learn a new Game Plan, a mental technology, that will allow you to unleash your greatest potential and enjoy yourself in the Process. You've followed us through Part I, 'The Opponent,' and Part II, 'Your Team.' Are you ready to dramatically enhance your performance results with the Perry Principles, in Part III, 'Your Game Plan?' "

He looked at us and smiled. "If you guys can do that for me I may even buy a few copies of this book for friends, just as long as they're not in the insurance business."

8

SURGE: RITUALIZE

(Sharpen Your Focus)

"Critical Carl, *Ritualize* is the first play in the Surge-Recover-Surge Game Plan. It's important and used frequently in sports because of its effectiveness both as a focusing technique and as a device for creating momentum into the Surge, into the actual performance itself. It has equal value in the context of business and serves exactly the same preparatory function." Critical Carl slowly nodded his head. I could see he had absolutely no idea what I was talking about.

"Look, it's really very simple. *Ritualize* means you create a specific repeating pattern of behavior prior to performance, a regular pretask routine, which sharpens your focus, concentration, and attention. When you Ritualize, your mind is cleansed of distractions while at the same time directed toward the specific task ahead.

"The ritual, your preplanned routine, is the most effective device for delivering yourself into the performance Process free from doubt, anxiety, and fear. In effect, it creates the perfect internal environment for summoning the Power of Hands-Free."

Creature of Habit and Ritual

In sports ritualization often involves a specific and meticulous ritual for putting on uniforms and equipment before competition. Jerry Rice of the San Francisco 49ers, the greatest receiver in NFL history, is extremely precise about his pregame preparation, the ritual. Rice has been called a creature of habit in this regard, but his habit is simply another name for ritual. Rice goes about his pregame business in a very studied manner.

Prior to every game, 49ers trainer Ray Tufts has Rice sit on the training bench while he carefully tapes the receiver's feet and ankles. Tufts does it in exactly the same way game to game, using virtually the same amount of tape and applying it in an identical way in a process that takes fifteen minutes.

Beginning with Rice's right foot, Tufts carefully wraps strips of white surgical tape around the foot and then up to and around the ankle in a ceremonial atmosphere where conversation is minimal and focus on the task is total.

Immediately following this taping session, equipment manager Ted Walsh very carefully spats the taped feet (i.e., imprints the Nike logo over the tape with special ink) making sure that the design is precise and neat. Rice abhors sloppiness in any area during his pregame routine including even something as insignificant as how the ink is applied to his taped ankles.

The NFL All-Pro then fastidiously dons his equipment and uniform, frequently glancing into a full-length mirror near his locker to ensure that there is no loose tape, that his handtowel is hanging at a specific location and length on his waist, that his wristbands are fitted in a precise and exact way, that his jersey is tucked in without being bunched up or wrinkled. Rice checks for and pulls off any loose threads he sees. He has even been known to send freshly laundered socks back to the equipment room if he felt they weren't quite right.

Rice immerses himself completely, almost obsessively, in his routine, the ritual, prior to every game. In fact, he is equally methodical, precise, and immaculate about his prepractice routine. Everything has to be and look a certain way, just right, to Rice before he goes onto the field. This is not a casual endeavor. Rice is meticulous, and he participates in the ritual with great conviction. He and other athletes and coaches understand its relevance.

Obviously, Rice's pregame ritual serves the practical purpose of protecting his ankles from injury, but equally

Even for scrimmages Jerry Rice is meticulous in his pregame ritual.

important is the fact that the routine sharpens his focus. It signals internally that his "game face," his competitive juices, must now come forth for the upcoming challenge. The ritual moves his attention from the general (which can often open the door to Polar Thinking and the Critical Advisor) and allows him to move seamlessly into the event.

Dallas superstar Deion Sanders goes to similar lengths as he gears up for optimum performance. Prior to all games Sanders has his entire uniform laid out on the floor of the locker room in exact replication of the way it will be worn, from cleated shoes up to his do-rag. From this point Sanders proceeds in carefully donning his equipment in a routine that brings his mind into a sharp focus.

Gladiator Mentality

Bill Walsh, former 49ers head coach and winner of three Super Bowl championships, calls this "the gladiator mentality." In analyzing it with us he observed how common the ritual was among athletes. "The [pregame] preparation, the ceremony, is part of the contest. There is a ritual, sort of a meditation during his [Rice's] routine, that develops for him the crescendo that takes him to the very peak of preparation. He's thinking, mentally focusing, as he goes through the ritual before the game. It draws him into the game."

Walsh himself had a routine he observed prior to competition, which he described for us. "I had a ritual that I did almost unconsciously, which involved how I went to my locker, how I walked through the room. Then I'd sit in the office and watch another game on television for five minutes. I walked out onto the field in a certain manner. As you prepare for a game there is a ritualistic state of mind that exists. The ritual helps you focus on what you are going to do."

Team Ritual

Teams also Ritualize. The 1995–96 NBA Champion Chicago Bulls developed a semiprivate ritual, or rite, they utilized before each game. During their record-setting 1996 season, gathering as a group, separate from the coaches, Scotty Pippen, Dennis Rodman, Michael Jordan, Bill Wennington, and the other team members put their hands together and performed a short team chant.

This ritual chant is understandable, since their coach, Phil Jackson, has used his knowledge and love of Indian culture at various times in coaching (the Lakota tribe gave him the warrior's name Swift Eagle when he conducted a clinic at their reservation). The six-foot-eight-inch Jackson invoked "the way of the warrior" and encouraged the team ritual because he understands its function and effectiveness.

The most outlandish member of the Bulls, Dennis Rodman, had his own preparatory ritual in addition to the team chant. The Worm, as Rodman is called, created his own cocoon of concentration before each game by sitting alone, eyes closed, listening to the rock music of Pearl Jam blasting out of his headset. Rodman was not doing this to kill time. He was involved in a routine, a ritual, that sharpened his focus and created positive momentum, drawing him into the game.

A Puzzled Critical Carl

I told Critical Carl from Cleveland all this. He smiled and asked, "I'm supposed to start taping my ankles before a sales call?"

"Only if it helps you start focusing on what you're going to sell," I replied.

"Very funny," he responded, "but what do Jerry Rice's taped ankles have to do with my selling insurance or a stockbroker's selling stocks?"

I cautioned him saying, "Be patient. You'll see."

The Comfort Zone

When you establish your own specific ritual prior to delivering a sales presentation, making a speech, or doing any other task, you have built an internal "comfort zone" which serves the same purpose it does for athletes; it allows you to have focused relaxation, to stay in the present as you move toward the execution of task.

The mental and physical activity of the ritual itself blocks doubt, anxiety, and fear while allowing you to build momentum in a positive internal atmosphere.

Critical Carl from Cleveland understood ritual in the context of sports easily enough, but he continued to have some difficulty making the transition to his own or other professions.

"Listen," I continued, "one of the most outstanding salespersons I've ever known, Thomas Rudwall of Provident Institutional Funds, used the telephone so effectively it was almost like a laser beam. And before he picked up the receiver he had a specific ritual he followed."

"Did it involve taping his ankles?" Critical Carl asked.

I smiled. "Pay attention. This could make you money. Rudwall routinely closes deals on the phone involving hundreds of thousands of dollars. In fact, more often it goes into the millions." I proceeded to explain Rudwall's ritual to Critical Carl.

Rudwall's Rewarding Ritual

Before making a sales call on the phone, Rudwall meticulously arranges his desk in the following manner. First he gets a fresh cup of coffee and places it on the upper lefthand corner of his desk. To his right he puts a blank tablet of yellow, narrow-lined legal-sized paper. Additionally he places two Bic pens (one red, one black) to the immediate right of the yellow legal tablet. Both pens point toward the bottom edge of his desk.

He then reviews the potential client's file, making relevant notations on the yellow legal pad that may include biographical, financial, or background information.

Following this he writes in bold letters three key points he intends to incorporate into the conversation. It may be financial information, national news that relates to the markets, or a specific mention of something from a previous conversation they had. This becomes a tangible resource if for any reason he is thrown off track during the call. Furthermore, he writes in red ink before the call and takes notes in black during the call.

Rudwall also tries to have a photograph of the individual he is calling available in the file. He looks at the photo and envisions that individual out in the backyard grilling hamburgers and wearing a chef's apron, hat, and mitts.

When he has carefully completed all of this, Rudwall pauses, slowly takes a sip of coffee from the cup on the upper lefthand corner of his desk, and then dials the client's number.

> *Repetition brings familiarity, and familiarity is the opposite of the unknown.*
> —STEVEN LEVENKRON

Rudwall always utilizes this specific ritual before important sales calls. It creates focus, momentum, and a comfort zone. Before he enters the unknown waters of the performance, the selling, he has settled into the moment with a ritual that seamlessly delivers him into the performance itself in the proper and most productive state of mind, a state of mind amenable to the Power of Hands-Free. And it is all totally within his control.

Unconscious Ritual

When we asked Rudwall where he had come up with the idea for doing all of this, his response was interesting. He said, "I just got into the habit of doing it over the years. I make lots of cold calls which are darn tough on the phone, and this just kind of made it easier to pick up the phone and just do it. That's why I like to briefly picture my customer making burgers. Kind of makes them more human, less threatening, a little more friendly in my mind.

"The whole routine gets me focused effectively. It keeps me pretty much thinking about what's happening right now instead of getting into what I call the 'fear scenario,' fretting about stuff I can't control." Of course, Rudwall unknowingly described a fear scenario that is created by Polar Thinking.

> *Most people confuse fretting with*
> *concentrating.*
> —ANONYMOUS

Rudwall had articulated the value of ritual beautifully. He had also developed it intuitively, or unconsciously, just as athletes such as Jerry Rice and others have done. However, ritualizing has equal value if you consciously develop your own preperformance ritual.

The reason ritual is so important when it comes to unleashing your best effort is that it's something totally within your control that you initiate and that blocks out Polar Thinking and the Critical Advisor.

When you prepare for any performance task, whether a speech, sales presentation, or any similar effort you greatly jeopardize your chance for success when you let Polar Thinking and the Critical Advisor take control and inject doubt, anxiety, or fear into your consciousness. By having a specific ritual you allow yourself to prepare in an atmosphere conducive to high achievement. To paraphrase Bill Walsh, the ritual draws you naturally and comfortably into the performance itself.

When Jerry Rice is highly focused on the wrapping of his ankles and meticulously putting on his uniform, he is taking control of what occupies his mind. Instead of worry or anxiety he has filled his consciousness with these simple acts. His conscious mind is totally absorbed with it, while his subconscious mind gears up for positive performance.

Rice has reduced fear of the unknown and installed a constructive routine, the ritual, just as Deion Sanders, the Chicago Bulls, or Thomas Rudwall do prior to performance. The ritual is the first step in creating an atmosphere conducive to surging on the Power of Hands-Free. The specifics of your ritual are less important than the creation of one you repeatedly utilize.

The Worm listens to Pearl Jam, and Rudwall gets his desk set up in a specific manner. A sales manager preparing for a meeting with his sales team might tape-record his comments in the car driving to work and then listen to the playback in his office before his presentation, taking notes of what he wants to emphasize. Your own specific professional responsibilities will help determine what works effectively in your own ritual.

Jerry Rice uses his ankle taping as part of the ritual. You may find that simply sitting in your car going over notes or a contract for five minutes prior to a meeting serves as a productive ritual.

However, as the great golf instructor Jim Flick told us during a putting instruction session, "Always have a specific routine you go through before you putt, but more important than the specifics of the routine is the preputt routine itself." Why? Because it draws you naturally and confidently into the Process.

The ritual is what brings your mind into focus on the task at hand and keeps the Critical Advisor at bay. An NBA player at the free throw line will go through exactly the same ritual every single time he shoots. The rituals differ from player to player, but they all have a specific free throw ritual.

Whether you're shooting a free throw or getting ready to sell insurance or institutional funds, give a speech, or do any other performance task, you'll gain an advantage through the ritual.

You must develop your own ritual. Create it. Believe it. Use it. It is the first play in the Game Plan for surging into the Power of Hands-Free.

SURGE: VISUALIZE

(Preview Your Performance)

I see a mental movie before I hit every shot.
—JACK NICKLAUS

I haven't been to a movie in years.
—CRITICAL CARL FROM CLEVELAND

The second powerful step in achieving optimum performance results is developing a keen ability to *Visualize.* Visualizing is a catalyst for getting in the Zone with the Power of Hands-Free, whether preparing for an important sales presentation, a speech, or a meeting to discuss a promotion.

Critical Carl from Cleveland was as skeptical about the need to Visualize as he had been of the necessity to Ritualize. "I'm pretty much a nuts-and-bolts kind of guy," he said. "That far-out New Age stuff isn't for me." I smiled because visualization is very much a nuts-and-bolts procedure in sports.

Goal getters like Jack Nicklaus know their ability to mentally rehearse, or "see" in their mind what they intend to do before they do it determines in large part whether they will do it. In effect, they train themselves to preview the performance mentally before it occurs.

These super achievers know if they allow their Critical Advisors to bombard them with excessive doubt, anxiety, and fear of failure, they greatly reduce their performance potential. They also understand that when they Visualize optimum Hands-Free performance, it becomes exponentially more likely to occur, for reasons we will describe. To put it another way, they know what you see is what you get, either good or bad.

One of the most dramatic examples of an individual's power to Visualize and the results it can produce occurred just before Super Bowl III.

"I Guarantee It!"

New York Jets quarterback Joe Namath stunned both the sports media and fans in Miami in 1969 with a "guarantee" of victory against the heavily favored Baltimore Colts. His fans, foes, and teammates didn't know what to make of it. Was Namath clowning, or was he crazy?

In spite of what thousands of so-called experts in the sports world were predicting (i.e., the AFC had been easily beaten in previous contests, and the Jets were eighteen-point underdogs, given no chance of victory) Namath was able to see the New York Jets as ultimate victors.

> *In order to be a leader . . . you have to make people want to follow you, and nobody wants to follow somebody who doesn't know where he's going.*
> —JOE NAMATH

When Namath guaranteed where he was "going," his teammates became believers in spite of the fact that in the days leading up to the contest, Broadway Joe was spending more time in nightclubs than he was on the practice field.

The final score was Jets 16, Colts 7. It was the first time an AFC team had ever won the Super Bowl. Sports history was made, and Namath became an instant legend in part because of his ability to Visualize. His mind had virtually created future reality.

Performers like Namath are aware of the remark "I'll see it when I believe it." For them the seeing is visualization. With positive mental rehearsal comes belief, specifically, belief in optimum performance results with what you focus on expanding (see Chapter 5).

Practicing in Your Mind

A less dramatic but more conclusive example of how effective visualization can be is the recent Harvard study concerning visualization. Two groups of amateur athletes were asked to practice shooting free throws twenty minutes a day for two weeks. The two groups were essentially equal in ability (i.e., minimal skills) when it came to shooting free throws at the start of the experiment as determined by results of testing.

At the end of the allotted two-week period they were again tested for shooting proficiency. Both groups had improved their percentages significantly and equally (over 20 percent). What is startling about the results is that one group had practiced each day with a basketball and regulation backboard and hoop. The second group had practiced without any equipment. The second group had simply visualized shooting free throws, while their counterparts were actually shooting them. The results were virtually the same. Visualization is a powerful tool.

Does the same thing happen in business and sales? Yes. Your ability to lead a sales team, motivate yourself, sell automobiles, or give a keynote address at a convention or service club is directly related to how you manage your mind when it comes to visualization. Visualization can have a profound impact on your confidence and subsequent performance results, but only if you understand what it is and how to use it correctly.

I explained all this to Critical Carl from Cleveland. Guess what. He continued to be skeptical (of course, skepticism and doubt are trademarks of the Critical Carls of this world).

Convincing Critical Carl

"Coach," Critical Carl grumbled, "I don't understand this whole Visualize thing you're talking about. I just don't get what it's all about." He was adamant and added for good measure and without smiling, "And just for your information, I'm not interested in learning how to meditate either." He was getting a little agitated.

I wanted to prove to Critical Carl that he was perfectly capable of visualizing and that he had been doing it successfully most of his life. I used one of my most effective demonstrations, which is usually effective because it involves a person of special importance.

Dear Old Mom

"Close your eyes and envision your mother's face," I gently suggested to Critical Carl. "How she fixed her hair, her favorite dress, her smile. Now recall her cooking and how she would prepare your favorite meal. The aroma of that meal would fill the kitchen and waft through your whole house. Maybe it was pot roast with potatoes and thick old-fashioned gravy, fresh corn, and homemade bread. Perhaps there was a fresh-baked apple pie on the counter in your kitchen back home."

I knew this was a very effective way to bring forth positive imaging that would serve as a perfect example of Critical Carl's ability to Visualize. It was such an obvious tactic and had worked so well in the past, I almost felt it was too easy. What happened next surprised me.

Critical Carl opened his eyes and began cursing. "@*%#!," he shouted, "my mother abandoned the family when I was just five years old! She was an alcoholic.

She ran around with other men and left my dad to raise four kids by himself!" he shouted. "Even now I can see her with a glass of Scotch in her hand and smell the cigarettes on her breath. And in addition to everything else she was a bad cook. There was no pot roast with potatoes unless it was on a tray in a TV dinner. I don't even want to think about my mother!"

I was shocked. This was not exactly the kindly image of Mom I had expected to invoke, and it startled me for a moment. "Sorry, Coach," he said, "but when you mentioned my mother all I could bring up in mind was a picture of her screaming at us kids and arguing with Dad. That was not a good time in my life."

Negative Visualization

I was silent until I realized he had made my point but in a rather circuitous manner. "Critical Carl," I said, "what you just did was a perfect example of visualization. You were able to see images in your mind that brought forth strong physical and emotional responses. In fact, your visualization was so powerful you could even smell cigarette smoke! However, what we are seeking is *positive* mental imaging, productive visualization. What you just did was the negative kind.

"Remember this, the Critical Advisor utilizes visualization just as the Power of Hands-Free does. However, the Critical Advisor uses it in a destructive manner by eliciting images in your mind of failure, loss, or other dire consequences. The reason why most individuals are adept at negative visualization, is that their Critical Advisors are in charge of their thinking. An amateur golfer will see his ball going into the sand trap. The professional golfer sees it going onto the green.

"You are typical of how most people use mental imaging. In fact, at one seminar I asked the audience to close their eyes and imagine a golf ball ten feet from the hole. Then I asked them to imagine themselves standing on the green getting ready to putt the ball. Finally I asked them to imagine themselves trying to sink the putt."

Critical Carl interrupted, saying "What's so difficult about that?"

I grinned because it confirmed what I had just suggested about the pervasive nature of negative visualization. "Half the group admitted they had missed the putt—missed an imaginary putt on an imaginary green where they had total control of the result! Even in a make-believe scenario, Polar Thinking and the Critical Advisor intruded and said, 'You are a bad putter. Who are you kidding? You can't make this putt!' "

The people at the seminar had total and absolute control over the outcome because it was occurring only in their imagination, but they came up with a negative visualization. And, of course, the truth is you don't have total control of the outcome if the Critical Advisor is in control.

What you're thinking, the shape your mind is in, is what makes the biggest difference of all.
—WILLIE MAYS

Top performers in sports have taken their own ability to Visualize and refined and directed it in a positive way with phenomenal power toward a specific target, namely, "seeing" what they want to do. They Visualize so repeatedly it becomes a habit, a very productive habit.

There are four steps to correct visualization, and we'll share them in a moment. But first, let's look at an explanation of visualization from a golfer who is generally regarded as the finest in the history of the game.

This explanation is appropriate here because it's as pure a description of how to Visualize correctly as anything we've ever heard. It also contains the four keys to successful visualization and will help you gain the ability to Visualize successfully.

At the Movies with the Golden Bear

With one hundred professional golf championships to his credit (including twenty Majors) and his recent victory in 1996's the Tradition, Jack Nicklaus has carved out a record that will probably stand forever in golf history. He is also the greatest moviegoer in the golf world. However, the movies the Golden Bear sees aren't the sort where you can buy a ticket, a box of popcorn, and a Coke.

Jack's movies are produced by Jack, written by Jack, star Jack, and are seen only by Jack. And, one other thing, Jack is always the winner in his films. Here's what he does.

In the words of Nicklaus, "Before I ever hit the ball, I see the result in my mind. It's exactly like a movie." This mental movie, is, of course, visualization as practiced by a master director.

Here's his detailed description: "I never hit a shot, even in practice, without having a very sharp, in-focus picture in my head. It's like a color movie. First, I see the ball where I want it to finish, nice and white and sitting up high on the bright green grass. Then the scene quickly changes, and I see the ball going there; its path, trajectory, and shape, even its behavior on landing. Then there's sort of a fade-out. The next scene shows me making the kind of swing that will turn the previous image into reality.

Jack Nicklaus: "I never in my entire life missed a putt in my mind."

Only at the end of this short, private Hollywood spectacular do I select a club and step up to the ball."*

Nicklaus sometimes refers to what he creates in his mind as a travelogue; he imagines exactly where he wants to go and what he will do to get there. And he recommends it for all golfers with one admonition, "Just make sure your movie shows a perfect shot."

If your own Critical Advisor just kicked in telling you "Yeah, but Nicklaus is the greatest ever. Besides, he's talking about golf. What's that got to do with you and your business?" The answer is "Everything!" starting with the fact that visualization is one of the reasons Nicklaus won one hundred professional tournaments.

What the Golden Bear (or Joe Namath or any other high achiever in sports) is doing by creating these vivid and positive mental pictures is preparing for optimum results with a process that jump-starts his performance.

Among other things, visualization actually produces a physiological change in the body. We saw it happen with Critical Carl from Cleveland when he started perspiring as he visualized his mother's image. Here's how it works.

Biofeedback in a Nutshell

We know that our brains produce measurable amounts of electrical current twenty-four hours a day and that those currents produce different patterns, or waves, depending on what we're thinking or dreaming about.

For example: Your brain waves look a certain way if you're being chased by a dog and another way if you're chasing the dog (the same can be said for the dog's brain waves). This can literally be seen and measured on an oscilloscope.

*Reprinted with the permission of Simon and Schuster from *Golf My Way* by Jack Nicklaus. Copyright © 1974 by Jack Nicklaus.

Your Celebrity Brain Wave

The most famous brain wave is the one scientists have dubbed the *alpha wave*. You hear so much about it whenever biofeedback is discussed because it shows up in a very particular and important situation, specifically, whenever you're focused, relaxed, self-confident, and creative. Please note these are the same emotions present when you are in the Zone, Surging on the Power of Hands-Free. It is this powerful and productive alpha wave mental state that you produce with positive visualization.

Think of Joe Montana driving the length of the field to win Super Bowl XXIII with less than two minutes left in the game—plenty of alpha waves inside that helmet. Think of Kenny G playing a great sax solo in concert—lots of alpha waves under all of that hair. And the same is true for any artist, athlete, or businessperson who gets into a peak performance mode, who gets in the Zone.

Jack Nicklaus's mental movie simply jump-starts the Process for him. His preview visualization is actually preparing the body for the task at hand, in effect, setting it up for optimum performance with a preperformance. The act of hitting a golf ball becomes just an extension of the positive visualizing that has been going on in his head. You've done the same thing without even realizing it. Let me prove it to you.

Free Biofeedback

If you're a golfer, bowler, tennis player, or other kind of recreational athlete, have you noticed what happens after you watch your favorite sport on television?

Let's say you watch some of the Masters golf tournament from Augusta on a Saturday morning before your own tee time. You see Fred Couples hitting a 275-yard drive with that effortless power he creates. You see Nick Faldo sink a smooth twelve-foot downhill putt and Davis Love III casually blast out of a trap to within ten inches of the cup.

You see other top pros set up, swing, and drive the ball down a beautiful, emerald-colored fairway. You unconsciously note the great care they take during competition, observing their actions and reactions, rhythms, and pacing.

Now, what usually happens when *you* go out to the course and play immediately afterward? That's right, your own golf game is a lot better! And the reason you play better is much more than simply coincidence. You just received a free biofeedback session courtesy of your TV. Your alpha waves were set in motion.

Jack Nicklaus is receiving a biofeedback session without the benefit of a television when he creates his mental movie. The same can occur for you when you apply mental movies to challenges in your business life, because visualization is a potent force when properly utilized.

Unfortunately, most people use the power of visualization against themselves. What they see produces the excessive doubt, fear, frustration, uncertainty, and anger that we saw in Critical Carl when he visualized his mother.

When your heart starts palpitating and your palms get sweaty before you stand up to give a speech, you're simply experiencing the results of powerful negative visualization. Polar Thinking and your Critical Advisor have taken control of your mental projector and are showing a horror film.

Here's how the super achievers direct the ability to Visualize so it creates enormous positive power that works for them, that allows the Power of Hands-Free to boost them into the Zone.

Four Keys to Successful Visualization

The four keys to your own powerful and effective visualization are very straightforward and are all in evidence during Jack Nicklaus's mental movie. The four keys are as follows:

1) **Focus on Process rather than prize.** Nicklaus focused just on performing or executing his next shot. He refused to allow his Critical Advisor to summon up a win-lose scenario in which he said something to himself like "If I hook it, I'll be out of bounds and lose the lead." He had the mental discipline and resolve (and it takes both) to keep his Critical Advisor in check. He did it by totally occupying his mind with seeing what he wanted to do next. He was playing to win rather than playing not to lose. The former creates confidence, energy, and direction. The latter produces fear, tension, and uncertainty. Whether you're making a sales call, giving a speech, or interviewing for a job, you must do the same, namely, see yourself in a successful performance mode without obsessive concern for the outcome. It takes practice, discipline, and strength; but top achievers accomplish it. Begin to Visualize like a top achiever.

2) **Get specific.** Including details in what you see creates a more powerful visualization. Nicklaus sees every element of the shot, including the bounce of the ball after it lands, the arc, the club head hitting the ball, and his actual swing. He wants to see as much of what he intends to do as possible. Remember his description of the ball? "Nice and white and sitting up high in the bright green grass."

See as much of your successful performance as you can including the exact words, facial expressions, colors, sounds, and movement. A well-known Chicago attorney actually goes to the empty courtroom the day prior to the start of a trial. He sits in a chair and sees the jury, the judge, the plaintiffs, the defendants, the opposing lawyer, and himself. His mental movie includes his opening statements. Thomas Rudwall includes visualization in his ritual prior to a sales call. A prominent Florida cosmetic surgeon sits in his office before a surgery and "sees" his patient's face as it will look after successful surgery. A popular history professor at the University of Wisconsin was once accused of napping before classes. The professor explained that his eyes were closed but his mind was open, seeing himself presenting the upcoming lecture with graphics, charts, and photographs. Ben Ailes, a successful California commercial photographer, has a photograph in his mind before he takes the picture. Regardless of your profession, when the task ahead is important, see yourself successfully doing it and you increase your chances of bringing it about.

3) **See perfection.** Visualize the task exactly as you want to do it. Nicklaus says, "I never in my entire life missed a putt in my mind." When you Visualize, be bold enough to see perfection because when your mind exceeds its limitations (Critical Advisor), your performance will reflect it. Recall past successes in similar situations and savor them. Draw strength, momentum, and belief in yourself from them.

4) **Visualize repeatedly.** Do it often! Do it on the way to work, in the shower, before you go off to sleep (be careful with that one—it may *keep* you from falling asleep), waiting in line. I repeat, repeat! Nicklaus claims he thinks about his swing off the course almost as much as he does on the course. The more your mind is occupied with positive images, the easier it becomes to perform them.

Preset for Performance

These four steps preset you for top performance results because the body responds to what is happening in your mind. There's something else that is important.

"Seeing" Is Believing

Skeptics say "I'll believe it when I see it." Such people need tangible evidence before they'll concede something is possible, whether it's reaching sales quotas, meeting deadlines under pressure, or winning a football game when their opponent is favored by eighteen points. Their minds are choked with the Language of Exclusion we described in Chapter 6, "The Leverage of Language"; and they labor under the enormous handicap of Polar Thinking.

They are the naysayers, the doubting Thomases who will give you fifty reasons things can't be done. They suck the life out of enthusiasm and destroy potential. Their Critical Advisors run amok.

Dress for Success

Top performers such as Jack Nicklaus know, "I'll see it when I believe it." They also know that belief precedes optimum performance, especially when the stakes are high.

For winners, that belief is the seeing that goes on internally. They see it in their minds before it actually happens, and it subsequently becomes much more likely to happen.

Nicklaus would do big things and little things to reinforce his powerful ability to Visualize. For example, the winner of the Masters is traditionally awarded a symbolic green jacket after walking off the eighteenth green Sunday afternoon. In his prime Nicklaus always took special care about what he wore on that final day. He recalls, "When I got dressed in the morning for that final eighteen holes on Sunday, I always wore clothes that would look good with green." Jack Nicklaus not only visualized for success, he dressed for success. It all goes together.

You can do exactly the same in preparing for and achieving important goals in your business and corporate life because the process is identical. Visualization is self-fulfilling.

> *In the province of the mind, what one believes*
> *to be true either is true or becomes true.*
> —JOHN LILLY

Critical Carl Versus Hands-Free

Critical Carl was uncomfortable with the concept of visualization and doubtful as to its usefulness in selling life insurance. He finally accepted it when I told him the fundamental reason his selling results were down was because he had unconsciously changed his visualization, from positive in the Power of Hands-Free to negative under the control of the Critical Advisor. Actually, he mentioned this change himself.

"You know, I've gotten to a point where I almost hate going in to make a sales call," he said. "I just don't have the confidence I used to have. Results have been bad. I know it's probably more of the same. I can almost see the scowl on a customer's face before I get to his or her office."

This was all I needed to hear, because Critical Carl had just informed me that his Critical Advisor was totally in control, beating him up mentally with negative visualization before his customers ever had a chance to do it. I said, "Can you imagine what would have happened if Jack Nicklaus 'just didn't have confidence' before he hit a shot, if he visualized a ball going into a sand trap instead of onto the green?"

Critical Carl needed to allow the Power of Hands-Free and its positive Visualization to take charge just as it had in his more successful years.

"Let me show you how to get your self-trust back so you can go into that sales call with only positive performance results in your mind," I told him. "Listen to this conversation between your Critical Advisor and the Power of Hands-Free, a conversation that probably occurred in your mind before your last sales call without your even being aware of it."

Getting Prepared for the Sales Call

Critical Advisor (CA): Well, you can't be looking forward to that meeting with Mr. Grigsby tomorrow. He's been avoiding you for weeks with every excuse you've ever heard. I don't think he'd be interested even if you offered him free life insurance.

Hands-Free (HF): Wait a minute! Hold everything! Mr. Grigsby probably is busy. After all, he is president of a successful trucking company that does over $20 million annually. So I view getting this meeting as the first success. After all these weeks and all those phone calls, he has finally decided to give me one of his most valuable assets, namely, his time. In doing that he has also given me a great opportunity.

CA: But it's not an opportunity of real value. He's already decided not to do anything but say, "No, thanks." I mean, look, he's only available for forty-five minutes, and that's just because you wore him down with your persistence.

HF: Forty-five minutes is more time than I need. In fact, I'll begin the meeting by telling him that it'll take less time than that unless he decides he wants to spend additional minutes evaluating my product. After all, it may be something that could provide greater protection for his family than what he has now.

CA: There's nothing Grigsby hasn't heard before. Nope, your little "less than an hour" offer won't fool him. I don't like the chances.

HF: I intend to go into that meeting and let him know that I respect his time. I will sit down and proceed with my agenda. I will let him tell me about what he already has. I want him to explain why he feels so comfortable. I will let him tell me why he thinks he has such a good policy and in doing that quickly ascertain where I can help him.

CA: You're not going to talk? Great! You're going to let Grigsby make the case that he doesn't need you? No way will that work.

HF: What I'm going to do is let him answer questions that I need to know before I can offer my most effective presentation. I've been in the insurance business for years, and I know from experience that I can help most of the people I deal with. I'm the expert on insurance. Mr. Grigsby is an expert on trucking. I promise you I'll be able to see very quickly if there is a service that I can provide for him.

CA: And if you can't?

HF: Fine. I know I can help most people. Mr. Grigsby may be in that other small percentage. But I do like my chances.

CA: Don't you think you're being a little too optimistic?

HF: I've been in this situation lots of times. Some of my best clients were more difficult than Mr. Grigsby, initially. Opportunity is all I ask. Mr. Grigsby has given me that great gift of opportunity, and I am very grateful. In fact, I am looking forward to doing what I do best, namely, selling insurance—specifically, selling life insurance to Mr. Grigsby. Believe me, it's gonna happen!

CA: You're not being very logical. In fact, you're basically dreaming. I don't think you'll be so optimistic after Grigsby says "Time's up. Adios."

HF: He's already said "Yes" once. I see him saying it again. In fact, I can already envision him behind his desk thanking me for opening up his thinking on the subject. He's apologizing for delaying our meeting so many times. Mr. Grigsby has a big smile on his face because I'm giving him information that will make his life better. He wants to know if I have time to set up another meeting next week with his wife and him. Critical Advisor, you may see this as an intrusion on Mr. Grigsby, something he wants to avoid. I see it as providing him with valuable information. And I want him to ask tough questions, because that means he's getting serious. In fact, I believe he was getting serious when he set up the appointment. I'm going to enjoy this.

CA: Not me. I'll be relieved when it's over.

HF: I'll be relieved when it starts because I will have succeeded in getting him to the table. I will have accomplished something very difficult. In fact, I believe getting in to see him is harder than anything else. After all, I have to get to him if I want him to understand the value of what I can bring to him. I want to get started. I envision a very successful meeting.

I looked at Critical Carl from Cleveland and asked, "Does the Power of Hands-Free or the Critical Advisor best reflect the kind of visualization that's going on in your head these days?"

Critical Carl forced a smile and said quietly, "I may be wrong, but it's probably the Critical Advisor."

Now I was getting irritated. "You *may* be wrong?" I said with too much impatience in my voice. "Critical Carl, your Critical Advisor has you so mixed up you're even uncertain about being wrong."

I added, "Did you notice that every single time the Critical Advisor spoke it was with the Language of Exclusion and that all he focused on, all he visualized, was failure? In doing that he sought out reasons to prove failure would occur because what you focus on expands." Critical Carl looked somewhat guilty as he slowly shook his head in agreement.

"Furthermore," I said, "did you notice how the Power of Hands-Free spoke only in the Language of Inclusion? Every thought he expressed and every image he created was directed toward proving himself right, and for the Power of Hands-Free that meant success. And, in addition to all of that he was absolutely enjoying the Process!

"The mental reality for the Power of Hands-Free was optimum performance, just like it was for Jack Nicklaus. And just like Nicklaus, the Power of Hands-Free used the keys to visualization. It focused on short-term performance rather than on possible negative results. It was specific in seeing the situation. It saw perfection, and it repeatedly envisioned success even though the Critical Advisor was bombarding it with so-called logical reasons for failure."

Critical Carl sadly shook his head in agreement and said, "That's how I used to be. I used to have the Power of Hands-Free."

I smiled. "Starting today, you're going to be like that again, Critical Carl, because the Power of Hands-Free is within you. We're going to bring it out so you can Surge on its tremendous positive force and get back on your game."

Critical Carl had a renewed sparkle in his eye, "Well, let's get started."

Surge: Optimize

(Turn It Up and Just Do It)

When preparing to perform an important task professionally, the moment arrives when it's time for you to ignite the performance fuse itself. Delay does damage.

When I told Critical Carl this, he nodded his head in agreement. "Coach," he said, "I've gotten so bad I'll do almost anything to avoid making the cold call—get coffee, organize my files, even open up junk mail. In fact, last week I started *reading* my junk mail!" I realized Critical Carl's two-option Polar Thinking had created a major-league procrastinator, afraid to step into the batter's box and take a swing at the ball, afraid to "just do it."

Practice, research, and experience are invaluable assets to have as part of your ongoing professional arsenal. However, at some point you must pull the trigger, or as the late revered golf instructor Harvey Penick advised, "Take dead aim." Penick's star pupil, two-time Masters winner Ben Crenshaw, summed it up this way: "You say that's a simple statement and it is, but it means so much more than that. It means trust yourself and not think about anything else." It means *Optimize*—turn it up and just do it!

Both Penick and Crenshaw knew performance potential is diminished when you allow yourself to find ever-increasing arguments for delays and postponements—to procrastinate. When you Optimize you allow yourself to trust in you and your capabilities, to have the self-confidence to pull the rip cord knowing the parachute will open. That big white billowing parachute is your optimum potential. It is achievement! Pulling that rip cord is to Optimize, to allow your potential to become reality.

Procrastination impairs this performance potential. Please note the difference between procrastination and prudence. To be prudent is simply to use good judgment, an asset of great importance in the context of successful performance results in business. But, as we saw earlier, our internal Risk-Reward Guidance System is thrown out of kilter by Polar Thinking. Polar Thinking and procrastination feed off and fuel each other. Procrastination allows Polar Thinking an opportunity to seep into your consciousness, which in turn allows your Critical Advisor even more opportunity to create doubt. We repeat, Polar Thinking breeds procrastination just as procrastination allows further Polar Thinking. It is a vicious and counterproductive circle that is eliminated when you Optimize.

Steak or Lobster? Lobster or Steak?

A condemned prisoner may take a long time deciding whether to order steak or lobster for his last meal. He or she understands that the executioner awaits and is in no hurry to proceed. In your own performance situation there is no executioner waiting (even though your Critical Advisor will tell you otherwise).

The procrastinators in corporate life who perform in the constrictive paradigm of Polar Thinking constantly see executioner waiting. They brood over and overevaluate each doubt and fear. They are simply stalling, and when they finally muster up the courage to act, they can see the shadows of the executioner on the ground coming up at them faster and faster—until it's too late. They waited too long to Optimize.

Turn It Up

Here are a few everyday examples of optimizing. You're driving down the freeway on a sunny day in July and a favorite Beatles song is on the radio. As "Penny Lane" comes out of the speakers, you grab the volume control and turn it up. Indecision? Unlikely. Further deliberation? Needless, of course. You simply turn it up!

When you read a new John Le Carre novel and it starts to get very intriguing, what do you do? Most likely you pull the book nearer to your face and get closer to the light!

When you see a family member for the first time after a long absence, someone you really love, what do you do? You run up and give him or her a great big hug!

Here's the point. When you want to enjoy the music, you turn up the volume; when you become absorbed in a book, you turn up the light and draw it closer to you; when you greet a person you really care about, you turn up the emotion. You Optimize.

And optimization is what ignites activity. Turn it up and just do it! Optimize! It's evident when Steve Young of the 49ers calls out over center, "Red 23, 14, hut, hut, *hut*!" Every San Francisco 49er on the playing field understands what happens after that last *hut*: Optimize; turn it up and get it done!

The great value of the first two Perry Principles, Ritualize and Visualize, is that they provide you with a self-controlled formula for creating positive momentum, which in turn enhances performance potential. They allow you to get ready to just do it in an internal atmosphere free from undue anxiety and fear, focused, self-confident, and ready to perform. These are fundamental elements present when you are in the Zone.

> *You must seek to have control and then act with abandon!*
> —ANONYMOUS

"Critical Carl, once your preparation has been completed (and it is completed when you Ritualize and Visualize properly), it is time to simply turn it up. Turn up the energy, the belief, the self-trust, and the emotion and Optimize! Athletes who play a sport that is under a time clock (football, basketball, hockey, etc.) have an automatic device that forces them to Optimize, the clock! When the referee's whistle blows, they turn it up and go at it. However, there is no referee's whistle in business, so procrastination is the norm, as in 'Let's put that off until later.' That's when you have to recognize the need to Optimize."

Critical Carl from Cleveland seemed to be getting the idea. "In other words," he said, "don't be afraid to get going on a project."

I noticed that even now Critical Carl continued to speak in the Language of Exclusion (i.e., he said "Don't be afraid . . ."). "Critical Carl," I asked, "do you mean 'trust yourself'?"

"You know what I meant," he argued.

Placing my hand on his shoulder, I looked at him and said politely, "Yes, I know what you meant and I know what you said, and they convey two different messages. 'Trust yourself' creates positive emotion and images and tells you what to do. 'Don't be afraid' is simply the Langauge of Exclusion, of avoidance. Critical Carl, will you do me a favor and read Chapter 6, 'The Leverage of Language,' again?" He nodded his agreement.

"Critical Carl, the fellow I told you about who used his phone like a laser, Thomas Rudwall, was successful in part because he knew how to Optimize. His ritualization and visualization concluded with that sip of coffee. That was the triggering mechanism to act. He was on automatic pilot at that point, prepared, comfortable, and confident. When he took that sip of coffee the performance fuse was ignited without effort, doubt, or fear. It triggered action. He Optimized."

Perls of Wisdom

The renowned psychologist Fritz Perls observed, "Human beings are the only species on earth who have the capability of interfering with their own growth." We see this evidenced in many ways (e.g., individuals with aggressive Critical Advisors are involved in self-thrashing most of their waking hours), but most visibly when the time comes to act, to turn it up and Optimize.

At the point of igniting performance such individuals interfere with their potential by refusing to trust themselves. Doubt dampens the performance fuse and inaction results. Using your ability to Optimize will break through procrastination and unleash your greatest performance results.

"Any questions, Critical Carl?" I asked.

"Tell me again. When do I know it's time to Optimize?" he said.

"You'll know," I said, "because you will first Ritualize, which flows directly into Visualize. After doing both you know it is time to Optimize, to turn it up and just do it. Ritualizing, Visualizing, and Optimizing become one seamless Process during which there is little chance for doubt, anxiety, and fear to creep into your preparation or performance. You become totally immersed in the activity itself or, as they describe athletes who are in the Zone, unconscious. Got it?"

> *It was just like when I was a kid shooting baskets. Just count 5, 4, 3, 2, 1, and go for it.*
> —KEVIN COSTNER, actor, star of *Tin Cup*,
> on how he won the chipping contest at
> the 3M Celebrity Challenge at Pebble
> Beach

Critical Carl signaled his understanding when he said, "Optimizing is when success becomes almost automatic?" He had nailed it.

"That's it. That's it exactly. The Ritualizing, Visualizing, and Optimizing put you virtually on a track toward optimum performance and then take you directly into the event or task itself, blocking out counterproductive distractions produced by Polar Thinking and the Critical Advisor. You have given yourself a formula that fuses you with the Process, the moment, the present. The formula is the crescendo Bill Walsh described, which takes you to a level of peak performance."

Critical Carl liked what he was hearing. "Beautiful, Coach. I like the Principles because they're as simple as A, B, C or, rather, RVOC!"

Surge: Capitalize

(Celebrate Your Success)

American film legends Clint Eastwood and John Wayne embody a long list of old-fashioned American attitudes and character traits in their various roles, in movies from *Dirty Harry* to *True Grit*. Courage, pride, fortitude, honor, and patriotism are just a few of them.

But like so many male American movie icons, both Eastwood and Wayne kept a tight rein on emotions that are still considered suspect in the corporate and business environment, namely, joy, excitement, enthusiasm, elation, or even outright happiness. In this specific regard they probably act on-screen about the same as you do at work.

Critical Carl heartily agreed with this idea. " 'Keep it to yourself' is my policy. I don't like a lot of emotion spilling out." By *emotion* Critical Carl meant positive emotion.

Macho Men Are Serious

Steven Seagal, Bruce Willis, Harrison Ford, Charles Bronson, Arnold Schwarzenegger, Sylvester Stallone, and most other movie "superheroes" continue to reinforce our antiquated notion that displays of the aforementioned attitudes (joy, enthusiasm, happiness, etc.) are less than macho. Rage is acceptable, as are extreme indignation, irritation, frustration, and apoplexy. It's OK to blow your top, boil over, seethe, and be enraged.

Female film stars are allowed more latitude when it comes to displaying positive and empowering emotions. Whoopi Goldberg, Jamie Lee Curtis, Jane Fonda, Candice Bergen, Geena Davis, Susan Sarandon, Jodie Foster, and their contemporaries are not charged with being macho. Thus their film characters frequently display positive reactions.

Win the battle, zap the evil genius, or blow up the opponent's entire army to save the world and our typical male

How to Capitalize? "Yes!"

"Critical Carl," I asked, "have you ever seen a film called *Home Alone*?"

He laughed, "Have I seen it? Only about five times. My kid, Mason, loves that flick."

Home Alone is one of the most popular movies of all time and stars Macaulay Culkin as a child, probably about Mason's age, who's left alone at home for several days. At the same time burglars decide to break into the house (of course, if they hadn't decided to drop by, the film's plot would have suffered).

I said to Critical Carl, "Culkin's character, Kevin McAllister, must fend off the aggressors with only his wits and ingenuity; and he *is* ingenious."

Critical Carl smiled. "Yeah, every time we see it I tell Mason, 'Hey, why can't you be like that kid?' "

I continued. "You'll remember that at one crucial juncture the robber sticks his head through the doggy door and says, 'Hi!' The youngster has anticipated this tactic and is lying in wait on the linoleum floor aiming a pellet gun directly at the robber's head at close range. Bang! The gun goes off, the robber is rebuffed, and Culkin has succeeded in defending himself against the odds.

"What is important in this example, Critical Carl, is the reaction demonstrated by Culkin's character. Do you recall his response? Did he sit there with a shy grin on his face and say, 'Aw shucks, it was nothin''? Did he frown and exclaim, 'Darn it, I only wounded him, so he'll probably come back'?"

"Coach, I loved his reaction," Critical Carl responded. "The boy's face lit up with a great big smile, his eyes got wide, and he clenched his fist and yelled, 'Yes!' In fact, the first time we saw it in a theater, the entire audience cheered along with him."

I nodded as Critical Carl described the scene. "What I really want you to remember," I added, "is that Culkin's character instinctively knew how to Capitalize on his strengths and his success. He took achievement and amplified it, pumped it up, for even more momentum. He knew how to celebrate his success! Kevin McAllister Capitalized."

Positive Energy Creates More Energy

His positive reaction is the image we want you to emulate in your own response to performance results. "Yes!" Be bold enough to show positive emotion and enthusiasm, to Capitalize, because in doing so you create a self-generating and productive force.

This will take some getting used to because those positive emotions are generally kept out of sight in the corporate environment. It is a much different situation when it comes to displays of negative attitudes.

When you're unhappy, angry, depressed, or just generally feeling out of sorts, it is commonly understood that it's more acceptable to manifest these feelings. Curtness, brusqueness, even the use of expletives are more in evidence as even your body language reflects your foul mood.

One of the reasons this is tolerated is because as we observed in Chapter 1, "The Paradox of Performance," pain is associated with productivity; if you are stressed out then you must be hard at work. Pain adds value. It is a badge, remember?

Of course, this idea is wrong. Constant criticism of yourself or others is as devastating to performance potential as self-approval is productive. The former is self-hurt. The latter is self-help. Nevertheless, the tyrant-boss is virtually a stereotype in our culture. The boss who is supportive, enthusiastic, comforting, communicative, and knows how to Capitalize is uncommon.

The tyrant is a powerfully suppressing force, just as the boss or coworker who knows how to Capitalize is a powerfully productive force. We incorrectly interpret the tyrant's behavior (or our own similar actions) as being that of someone who is working hard. Thus the tyrant's behavior is often tolerated instead of being viewed as damaging.

While the character in *Home Alone* is fictional, the behavior characteristic he demonstrated, Capitalizing, is real and can serve as a valuable example for you to emulate.

Connors Can Capitalize!

"You see athletes who know how to Capitalize all the time in sports, Critical Carl. In fact, Jimmy Connors's trademark was pumping his fist in the air after a great point. You could just see him increasing his positive momentum."

Critical Carl supplied his own example. "Hey, Connors may have started it, but the person who is maybe the greatest female tennis player in history did the same thing. When Martina Navratilova ruled the tennis world, she would pump her fist and let out a shout of joy after a big point. You could almost see her increasing her own momentum."

I agreed. "Navratilova was simply amplifying her success. She was acknowledging positive effort and achievement and capitalizing on it.

"The best evidence of what it means to Capitalize, however, may occur in basketball when a player goes to the free throw line. The next time you watch a game, pay

Connors loved to Capitalize.

attention to what happens after a player takes his first free throw at the crucial moment in the fourth quarter."

"Coach, I know what you're gonna say," he answered, "After he shoots a free throw, regardless of whether he makes it or not, other players will immediately come over and give him a pat on the butt and some words of encouragement—maybe just a positive nod of the head."

"That's right, they are offering support, encouragement, and positive emotion," I answered. "Imagine the impact it would have on a player if he knew his teammates would scowl and criticize him for missing a free throw that he had tried desperately to make."

Critical Carl shook his head. "Come on, Coach, that would never happen. It would have a terrible effect on the player at the free throw line."

"Exactly right," I replied, "just as it would have a negative impact if there was little or no reaction when he successfully made the shot."

And what is important to understand is the same thing happens in business when you withhold support from yourself and others, when you are reluctant to Capitalize. You damage your potential just as a team would hurt themselves by withholding positive input from a player at the free throw line.

A lawyer who wins a judgment might Capitalize (waiting until she's out of the judge's chambers, of course). An automobile dealer who sells a new car (or even a rusty used car) can Capitalize and allow himself a "Yes!" once the customer has exited. An account executive at an advertising agency who is awarded a new ad campaign can Capitalize with high fives around the office. An acquisitions editor at a publishing company who sees a successful final draft of a book she helped procure can Capitalize with an internal or external round of applause for herself. And so can you when you achieve successes either large or small.

That success is raw fuel. It is ignited when you Capitalize to help yourself achieve even greater success.

Athletes have a profound understanding of this. A basketball team will Capitalize whether a teammate sinks the free throw or misses it. They know he gave 100 percent in trying to make the shot. They want to help instill confidence, focus, awareness, and relaxation for the next shot, the next performance. Capitalizing does this. It's the norm in sports and the exception in business even though it is equally valuable in both.

A typical executive will take success and quickly put it in his or her pocket with little notice. A lawyer who receives a positive judgment in a ruling will let it pass with minimal reaction. A doctor whose seriously injured patient survives will simply move on to the next seriously injured patient without taking a moment to Capitalize. A corporate accountant who successfully survives an IRS audit will simply breath a sigh of relief (à la Troy Aikman) rather than really celebrate the success.

Instead, it is the setback, the failure, the downturn that creates emotion—all negative. It's what we mean when we say most adults Capitalize on their weaknesses and setbacks. Doubt, anxiety, and fear are the weaknesses that they amplify instead of the successes.

> *My dad was gone a lot . . . so my mom was there to help me celebrate when I had a good game.*
>
> —CAL RIPKEN JR., baseball superstar

Mrs. Cal Ripken's positive input, her ability to celebrate with her young son, is the essence of what it means to

Capitalize. It is the difference between Clint Eastwood's (Dirty Harry's) nonresponse to success and Macaulay Culkin's (Kevin McAllister's) positive reaction. The unabashed enthusiasm of Culkin, Cal Ripken Jr.'s mother, Jimmy Connors, or any basketball team in the country, men's or women's, is the model to keep in mind. It will pay big dividends.

Critical Carl and I discussed this. Then he smiled. "I guess if Charles Barkley can bring himself to pat a teammate on the back, so can I."

"Remember yourself," I added. "Remember to pat *yourself* on the back. That's where it has to start."

Be Your Own Best Fan

Tegla Loroupe, a world-class distance runner, understands the value and need for supporting, encouraging, and applauding your own efforts and achievements. In 1994 she became the first black African woman to win a major marathon by triumphing in the New York City Marathon. She won again in 1995 just days after the sudden death of her sister.

Her accomplishments are all the more astonishing because the Kenyan society in which she was raised actively discouraged women from competing in sports, ignoring their accomplishments and withholding rewards. So, says Loroupe, "If no one gives you encouragement, you have to encourage yourself." That encouragement comes when you Capitalize.

Critical Carl was beginning to understand the importance of being able to Capitalize, being able to give himself (and others) the freedom to celebrate success and even the effort to achieve success. However, he looked troubled about something. "Coach," he asked, "this is all good when things are working out swell and you have something to celebrate, when you're Surging. But what happens when you fall out of the saddle and suddenly you can't buy a break? When you've lost or think you'll probably lose? What then?"

I smiled and said, "Remember our goal is to Surge on the Power of Hands-Free, which is what RVOC enables you to consistently accomplish. It sets you up in an ongoing mode of high performance. But when you run into trouble, fall out of the saddle, you need to Recover quickly. That is the key, quick recovery.

"When the Critical Advisor leaps into your consciousness with doubt, fear, anxiety, anger, sadness, guilt, or any of the negative emotions, perspectives, and attitudes it has at its command, you are ripped out of the present, out of the Process of performance.

"When this happens there are specific questions you must ask yourself to prevent your being swept away by their force. These questions are the final Perry Principles and will help you *Recover* from Polar Thinking and your Critical Advisor for a quick return to the Power of Hands-Free."

RECOVER: NOTICE

(The Awareness Question)

Ask: "What am I Noticing?"

Earlier we cautioned that while *In the Zone*'s Game Plan is designed to be easily and productively incorporated into your life, there are two elements requiring special patience and effort. One, you'll remember, involves removing the decades-old barnacles of the Language of Exclusion while at the same time learning to flex the muscle of the Language of Inclusion.

"I'm gonna work on using inclusionary language, Coach. Breaking old habits is tough," Critical Carl said.

"That's right," I replied, "and the principle we're going to present now will be equally challenging and perhaps even more valuable. That principle is developing your ability to be keenly aware of your attitudinal and emotional responses to setbacks, obstacles, challenges, or imagined results immediately when they arise. It is challenging because these negative reactions occur reflexively and consume us before we realize it."

Emotional Awareness

The challenge is to become aware of that which happens unconsciously and spontaneously. It has been likened to trying to stop a sneeze while you are sneezing.

An early warning or red flag system of self-awareness is crucial at these times, because left unchecked the emotions that are released by Polar Thinking boot you out of the Process, out of the present where your power is, and into the future or past where the Critical Advisor lurks waiting to damage your performance. It will have taken you out of the Process before you know what's happened and will keep you diverted until your performance potential is destroyed.

This, of course, is the conundrum—to become aware of that which happens spontaneously or unconsciously. It means you must monitor yourself at those times when it is most difficult, when you're consumed by doubt, anxiety, tension, anger, guilt, sadness, or any of the other counterproductive feelings and reactions your Critical Advisor summons up. When this happens all else is bulldozed from your consciousness. Those bad feelings become your consciousness at the great expense of your performance and its potential.

Thus, when a person is overcome by a particular emotion (e.g., anger) he or she is said to have lost it. What they have lost is control of the present, the now.

Stubbing Your Toe in the Process

"Critical Carl," I suggested, "let's say you're watching a football game on television, and it's Miami against Dallas. Miami is coached by Jimmy Johnson, who was fired by Dallas owner Jerry Jones even after Johnson had won two Super Bowls at Dallas. In other words, there is lots of bad blood between these two guys and it's reflected in a great hard-fought game.

"The score is tied at seventeen-all in the fourth quarter, when they take a commercial break with under two minutes left. Suddenly you remember there's a quart of Ben & Jerry's Cherry Garcia ice cream in the freezer and race out to get it. On the way to the kitchen you stub your toe hard—I mean really hard—on your son's bicycle, which he had left in the dining room.

"As that big jolt of pain shoots up to your brain from the stubbed toe, you grab your foot and let loose with some choice words, correct?" He nodded in agreement.

"OK, now please observe in this example that while you are hopping up and down, angry, impatient, and yelling, you, Critical Carl, have been thrown out of the Process. Your Critical Advisor halts the Process of your getting the

Ben & Jerry's Cherry Garcia ice cream. Your Critical Advisor's automatic and unnoticed emotional outburst creates additional problems. For example, when you race to the refrigerator you drop the ice cream on the floor as you try to make up for the lost time, you knock the ice cube tray on the floor accidentally in your flustered rush, or you stub the toe of the other foot in your hurry to get back to the Dallas–Miami game before the commercial ends.

"Ultimately the most damage may come from actions resulting from your unchecked negative emotions rather than the original incident."

Critical Carl from Cleveland started at me. "So?" he asked.

I continued. "Just this. When you stub your toe professionally the same thing happens. While you're lost in pain induced by Polar Thinking and your Critical Advisor you are immobilized, thrown out of the Process; and your performance in the present is diminished.

"Remember, when you surge on the Power of Hands-Free you are completely within the Process of "doing," whether it's planning or executing a specific task such as getting ice cream, selling insurance, evaluating a mutual fund, or giving a speech. And while it would be wonderful to be constantly Surging with top performance, unfortunately, this is rare.

"Instead we occasionally stub toes, suffer loss, are rebuffed, question ourselves, or worry about future results either good or bad. And when this happens we must recover quickly or our difficulties are compounded. In order to recover we must first *Notice* that we are being swept away in emotions that range from doubt to rage and everything in between.

Critical Carl smiled. "In other words, whether I'm upset about stubbing my toe or really stressed about losing an important sale, when I let my Critical Advisor's negative emotions or feelings take over, I hurt myself."

I nodded. "Especially if you let them go unchecked! That's when the real damage occurs."

All Tied Up

It can happen to a major-league ballplayer who goes into a slump and extends it by letting anger, consternation, or extreme doubt play on his mind ("Will I ever pull out of this thing?"). His emotional upheaval makes it even more difficult to get back on track. The expression "all tied up in knots" describes it well. The ballplayer's Critical Advisor is the one tying him up. He becomes so concerned about getting out of the slump that it only gets worse.

It can happen to you when suddenly sales disappear. You push harder and harder with less and less to show for it. Your mood darkness, your performance suffers, and you get diminishing results. You are completely unaware that it is even happening. It can happen to a lawyer whose motion is denied by a judge, a graphic artist whose new computer design work is rejected, or a stockbroker who is losing clients. The setback is less a problem than the unobserved reaction to it.

The Daze

It happened to golfer Corey Pavin amid the Georgia pines and blooming azaleas at Augusta on a gorgeous Sunday afternoon in April during the final round of the 1986 Masters. The five-foot-nine-inch, 150-pound Pavin, whose nickname is Bulldog, eagled the par-five fifteenth hole to get within one shot of the lead. He was suddenly in position to win golf's biggest event, in the hunt for a coveted green jacket and piece of golf immortality.

Pavin, perhaps the game's greatest pure shot maker, walked briskly to the sixteenth tee, a 170-yard par three, and pulled out a five iron in preparation for the final three holes and what he hoped would be a continuation of his outstanding play. He was pumped up and eager to get on with it—too eager as it turned out.

Instead of a continuation of fine play, the shot coming off his club was a horrible misfire that plopped into the water running alongside the fairway and up to the sixteenth green. This error immediately erased his great performance on the preceding hole and jeopardized his chances for victory. The shot was an obvious choke.

Pavin was devastated. He knew he had choked and that Jack Nicklaus was making a charge a hole or two back, eliciting cheers from the crowd with outstanding shot after outstanding shot.

Pavin, now distraught and unfocused, sat down on a bench with his face in his hands, wallowing in the negative emotion brought on by his Critical Advisor's self-recrimination, sadness, and anger. He later described himself as being swept away "in a daze." He had lost it—the present—in a rush of negative feelings following his choke. He said he felt as if it were "the end of the world."

Pavin's Critical Advisor was screaming at him loud and clear, chastising him severely immediately after the five-iron misfire. What made it fatal in golf terms was that he was so caught up in the self-administered bashing he didn't Notice it was even happening. In addition to the problem of the immediate past (hitting a five iron into a water hazard), he was now in the process of destroying the present and future by allowing his Critical Advisor to have complete control.

And so, the tournament was over for Pavin. He shot a five on the sixteenth hole and bogeyed the eighteenth. His *response* to the setback (i.e., stubbing his toe professionally) rather than the setback itself knocked him out of the tournament. The emotional toxins spewed forth by Pavin's Critical Advisor were overwhelming and rendered him helpless because he had been unable to regain control.

Noticing Puts You Back in Control

You begin to regain control when you force yourself to Notice, to be aware of your reactions. While this is very difficult, it's the first and most vital step if you are to quickly Recover.

When the Critical Advisor fills your consciousness with anger, frustration, concern about great gain or loss, trepidation, or any other counterproductive emotion as it had done to Corey Pavin, control has been taken away from you. Your rational thought process has been replaced by the "daze" in one variation or another. The present, the Process, the moment, the performance, has been lost. Or, more accurately, it has been stolen—stolen by your Critical Advisor.

The Awareness Question

The first step in the Recover process then is to seize control from your Critical Advisor and get back into the present. You do this by honing your self-awareness—by Noticing. When your Critical Advisor creates doubt, anxiety, fear, or any negative response or counterproductive emotional reaction in your consciousness, a mental red flag must immediately go up alerting you to this change. You must instantly see the Critical Advisor (that angry and bullying creature we asked you to create at the end of Chapter 3) and understand you are under direct attack by this enemy within. (One of the reasons we asked you to be conscientious and detailed in painting a mental picture of the Critical Advisor is that it helps you quickly identify the presence of negative emotions if you see an actual presence or entity. It is easier to fight this creature than an amorphous rush of emotions. The struggle becomes one against this tangible opponent, the Critical Advisor, rather than against the feelings it produces.)

When you lose a sale, miss a deadline, have an argument with an associate, worry about an upcoming performance review, prepare for a sales presentation, or face any of many other challenges, setbacks, or failures, your internal red flag identifying the Critical Advisor is your early-warning system. In spite of the mental anguish, the reflexive plain, you must immediately ask yourself the first transforming question in the recover formula, "What am I Noticing?"

"What Am I Noticing?"

When you answer the question, "What am I Noticing," it is almost irrelevant what you Notice (e.g., "I'm extremely disappointed," "I am very stressed about the upcoming meeting," "I am getting very frustrated with my lack of results," "I am very angry at myself," or any other observation that begins your internal examination of what you are Noticing), because by simply asking yourself the question and then considering and answering it appropriately, you have seized control of your consciousness from the Critical Advisor. You are in the Process again.

Please know that you must ask that specific question rather than "How do I feel?" or "How am I doing?" both of which can be answered perfunctorily and without much thought, "lousy," "terrible," or "horrible."

The pivotal question to ask to start to Recover is "What am I Noticing?" because you are forced to give it due consideration. It requires a more involved response, one that holds you in the present for a longer period (so be absolutely sure you give a meaningful and complete response). Truly engage the question, because in so doing you calm down the Critical Advisor, keeping it at bay while holding yourself in the present.

You must be determined and disciplined enough to raise the red flag and cut through the automatic emotional daze (i.e, the anger, despair, disappointment, etc.) and become aware that you are caught up in it. Noticing what is happening emotionally immediately will have an impact on what you do next, whether you're making a sales presentation, giving a speech, writing a legal brief, or finishing the final, deciding holes at the Masters.

Pavin Learns to Notice

The Corey Pavin story does have a happy ending. While the Golden Bear went on to win his sixth Masters championship the year of Pavin's collapse in 1986, Pavin continued to persevere after learning a valuable lesson at Augusta. Pavin understood (and said publicly) that although his uncontrolled despair and anguish were honest reactions to the failure on the sixteenth hole, they were the wrong reactions. He understood that he should have fought to regain his composure and prepared for his next shot. As every golfer knows, a lot can happen (good and bad) on the last two holes on the final day at the Masters. Instead, Pavin lost control and had no device for reclaiming it.

Pavin could have given himself a chance to win if he had trained himself to Notice.

Pavin Gets Noticed

By 1995 Pavin had become known as the greatest golfer never to have won a major, a backhanded compliment with odious connotations (read "chokes under pressure"), but he continued to work on his mental skills.

At the '95 U.S. Open at New York's extremely demanding Shinnecock Hills, Pavin was once again in contention coming down the stretch. This time a different but equally formidable presence was lurking just behind him, namely, the Great White Shark, Greg Norman. In fact, Pavin was more than in contention. He arrived at the seventy-second and final hole with a fragile one-stroke lead over Norman.

As Pavin looked forward from the eighteenth tee, he saw an exceptionally tough 450-yard hole extending straight out from the tee box and then swinging uphill and left to a rolling green that was protected by bunkers and thick rough. For a relatively short hitter like Pavin, this hole presented an inordinate test of both his mental and physical skills.

After going through his preshot routine, the Ritualization and Visualization, Pavin Optimized and unloaded a dead solid perfect drive that faded beautifully down the right-center of the eighteenth fairway 210 yards from the pin. With Norman now staring out from the eighteenth tee directly behind him, Pavin understood the significance of his second shot. If he hit the green and made par he would win the tournament (unless Norman made a very improbable birdie).

However, if Pavin stumbled as he had done at Augusta in 1986, Norman could win the tournament with a birdie or force a playoff with a par. Realistically, Pavin knew the U.S. Open was probably his to win or lose.

Thus, this second shot became pivotal. Pavin, after careful deliberation, selected a four wood, and addressed the ball. He then executed what is considered to be one of the greatest pressure shots in golf history, a beautiful low, hard draw that honed in directly at the pin.

Pavin was ecstatic, and to the astonishment of viewers around the world, began *running down the fairway* chasing after the golf ball while it was still in the air! Because Pavin was among athletes known for their stoicism, this extraordinary outburst was akin to seeing your grandmother line dancing at a local tavern.

And then, just as suddenly, Pavin stopped and knelt down on one knee, bowing his head for almost fifteen seconds. Pavin told reporters later he was simply regaining control of the moment, removing excessive and potentially disruptive emotions, something he hadn't done at Augusta in 1986. Now he intended to stay focused in the Process and understood that Capitalizing or celebrating before he had completed his task, which was to make par, was premature and potentially damaging to his concentration and subsequent performance.

At Augusta in 1986 Pavin's emotional upheaval and unawareness, the negative daze, had taken him out of the tournament with two holes remaining. In 1995 Pavin was accomplished enough at self-awareness, or Noticing, to ensure that he would remain in the Process until the final hole was completed. He would correctly Capitalize at the conclusion of his task rather than during it. (Professional golfers are notorious minimalists when it comes to Capitalizing, or celebrating, both for reasons of etiquette and because they understand that the continuum of a round of championship golf requires great emotional equanimity. Thus displays of positive emotion are usually seen only

Will Tiger Woods stop Capitalizing now that he's a pro?

after the last putt on the last hole *if* it results in a championship. Even at the highest levels, golfers would benefit if they would allow themselves the freedom to Capitalize in an appropriate manner more frequently. One important exception is America's Tiger Woods, who won his third consecutive United States Amateur Championship in 1996. Woods, the first person in history to do this, aggressively pumps his fist after making a crucial putt in a manner that is reminiscent of Jimmy Connors. It is a tremendous asset to the young golfer and one that will undoubtedly be greatly reduced now that he is a pro.

Pavin meanwhile calmly arose from one knee and strode up the incline to the green where with two putts he claimed his first-ever Major, the 1995 United States Open. He had learned a valuable lesson the hard way nine years earlier. Pavin had trained himself in his own manner to Notice, to get back in the present, the Process, and regain control.

Noticing Returns Control to You

Noticing is your key to getting back to the present and regaining control. The emotions we must conquer are those that take us out of the Process and unconsciously sweep us up as they did to Pavin at the 1986 Masters and almost did to him on the final hole of the 1995 U.S. Open.

When counterproductive emotions arise we must prevent ourselves from being jerked out of the Process. Please note that in 1986 negative emotions destroyed Pavin's focus. In 1995 positive emotions threatened him (elation at his tremendous second shot under enormous pressure while he still had critical putts immediately ahead). We must be alert to both, because either can shatter the Process.

Ask the Question

I looked at Critical Carl and said, "Asking yourself, out loud if necessary, 'What am I Noticing?' when that red flag goes up in your mind is the catalyst for reclaiming control of the present."

Critical Carl looked a little bemused and said, "You're right. It is almost like trying to stop sneezing in the middle of a sneeze."

"It takes determination," I continued, "but you can do it. This is where the real battlefield exists, when your focus and concentration are removed from the Process. If you regain it, you're back in the saddle. By asking this question, 'What am I Noticing?' you have seized control from your Critical Advisor. You are back in the Process, back in charge. Corey Pavin was unable to do it in the '86 Masters but had greatly improved his emotional self-awareness by 1995. When he Noticed his emotions taking him out of the Process, he had the strength to successfully regain control. It may have been responsible for his winning the U.S. Open."

Critical Carl nodded his head approvingly. "And by finally winning his first Major, he got the monkey off his back, right?"

"That's right, but Pavin made a very astute observation regarding that. He said, 'It's good to get the monkey off my back about the Majors, but it was my own monkey that I put on my own back.' He understood that ultimately we control whether or not we succumb to pressure, stress, outside expectations, or other Polar Thinking obstacles. And it's within our own power to successfully eliminate them, to get the monkeys off our backs. You see, the monkey is created by your Critical Advisor."

RECOVER:
OPTIONS-LEARNING

(The Empowerment Question)

Ask: What are my Options,
and what am I Learning from them?

When your attitudinal or emotional red flag goes up and you quickly ask, "What am I Noticing?" You have wrested back control of the present from your Critical Advisor. You must next consolidate and extend that control by asking yourself, "What are my *Options*, and what am I *Learning* from them?"

I explained this to Critical Carl and he was curious. "What's the point of asking a two-part question?" He addressed an important issue.

"Critical Carl," I replied, "the first part of the question, 'What are my Options?' is the jackhammer you use to break apart Polar Thinking by creating multiple Options, choices other than win-lose. The second half of the question, 'What am I Learning from those Options?' uses the newly created alternatives as a source for gaining information and, more important, self-trust. As you'll see, information and self-trust are intrinsically connected to your ability to Recover.

> *If behind in the second half because your*
> *running game has stalled, switch to your*
> *passing game.*
> —JOHN WILLIAM HEISMAN, creator of the
>   Heisman Trophy

First, you must create *multiple* Options to remove the fear induced by Polar Thinking's two-option format, a format extremely detrimental to your performance potential.

Remember, the goal is to perform at your best with the Power of Hands-Free, but when you stub your toe either professionally or personally, it's imperative to Recover quickly. This is extremely difficult if you believe you have failed, as we saw evidenced by Corey Pavin's reaction on the sixteenth hole of the Masters. He virtually declared himself the loser because of Polar Thinking and his subsequent inability to Recover.

Pavin was paralyzed because in his (Polar Thinking) view, he had failed. This is just as damaging to performance potential as the fear of failure. Both destroy your control of the Process, and both emanate from Polar Thinking and the Critical Advisor.

Thus when you regain control of the moment by asking "What am I Noticing?" you must then immediately remove Polar Thinking's continuing win-lose threat by creating additional Options. These new alternatives eliminate the win-lose threat of the competition that exists in the form of failure or potential failure.

Please observe that instead of suggesting that you remove the contest, we say you must remove the threat of the contest, a threat created by Polar Thinking's win-lose format.

While the competition obviously remains in sports, business, and life, the menace it poses in your mind can be greatly lessened when you erase two-option Polar Thinking from your consciousness. You remove it quickly by creating multiple outcomes, choices, and interpretations. You remove it by asking yourself, "What are my Options?"

Action Options

The Options you develop must be action oriented and present positive alternatives that move you from being a passive victim of your Critical Advisor to once again being an active participant in your own success and the Power of Hands-Free.

Suppose Corey Pavin noticed his extreme negative emotion, the daze created by his Critical Advisor, and quickly asked, "What are my Options?" He would have informed himself that the 1986 Masters was still in progress and that he was still viable, that Jack Nicklaus and the others could yet stumble and he, Pavin, had two holes remaining to try to win the championship—a positive perspective on his situation.

He then may have identified as his action Option a dependable swing thought ("Keep my head steady," "Slow on the backswing," or "Swing through the ball") for his next shot in an attempt to get that shot close to the pin to salvage the hole.

He would then totally immerse himself again in the Process of the Surge Game Plan, RVOC, in preparation for that upcoming shot and a return to the Power of Hands-Free.

Pavin's reaction to the errant five iron on the sixteenth hole took him out of the tournament. His own Critical Advisor became a tougher opponent than any player out on the course. It became his judge, jury, and executioner just as it does for you. And, with the Critical Advisor, you can be assured the verdict will always be "Guilty!"

A teacher who is having difficulty getting the full attention of a class over several days would develop Options. He might ask himself, "Should I invite more questions from the students?", "Will guest lecturers get their attention?", or "Should I get out from behind the lectern and move around more while I speak?"

Rather than simply writing off the class as hopeless and his work as a failure, the teacher should ask, "What are my action Options?" and then establish what they are.

A stockbroker who finds her client list diminishing might review her procedures for gaining new clients and compare it with the past. She might discuss with associates who are having better results what they view as important to their success. She could read material relevant to her business and the problems she is facing or discuss with investors who are friends what they view as important qualities in the broker they do business with.

But regardless of whether you are a sales executive, teacher, insurance salesperson, stockbroker, or other professional, you can absolutely refuse to simply suffer in silence while Polar Thinking and your Critical Advisor administer continual self-bashings. Seeking multiple Options for action is preferable.

I explained this to Critical Carl. He was eager to address this point. "Coach, here's the problem. When I am getting ready to deliver a speech, I understand perfectly well that I'm either going to somehow stumble through it without looking too much like a fool or, more likely, screw things up and sound stupid. That's the reality. It's all or nothing, and the nothing is more likely."

A Room with Just Two Doors

Critical Carl was articulating the perspective that inhibits performance in all areas of life, whether it's athletics, selling, public speaking, fine arts, or motivating and believing in yourself.

Polar Thinking puts you in a small, dimly lit room, poorly ventilated and without water or electricity. It is a windowless room with only two doors. Behind one of the doors is possible success. Behind the other door is total failure. Believing you must walk through one of those two doors during your performance without knowledge of what awaits you sets loose your Critical Advisor. To allay the fear, doubt, and anxiety the Critical Advisor causes, you must construct additional doors, psychological exits. You do this when you ask yourself "What are my Options?"

"Critical Carl," I said, "you have restricted yourself even further; both of your doors offered Options that were bad, either 'stumble through and somehow not look too much like a fool,' or 'screw up and sound stupid.' You have virtually removed success from your paradigm. You went fur-

Polar Thinking has just two doors. One of them is failure.

ther than Polar Thinking and saw only one door you could walk through, failure! Many of us do the same thing. We say 'I never have any luck with that account,' 'I can't win for losing,' or, 'Just my luck.' We reduce our possible outcomes to one, namely, failure."

The two Options of Polar Thinking do almost the same thing. When faced with a stark success-failure scenario, your attention usually gravitates toward failure.

A Room with More Doors

You must give yourself more exits, more possible outcomes, interpretations, or alternatives so the feeling of pre- or postperformance claustrophobia or "psycho-cramps" that Polar Thinking produces in a "room with two doors" is eliminated.

If Polar Thinking and the Critical Advisor appear before performance (e.g., while you're preparing for an important sales presentation, speech, courtroom presentation, or other task) and produce doubt, anxiety, and fear, you must immediately notice or red flag it and create multiple Options that offer additional "exits."

Those action Options might include seeking advice from others you respect in the area, whether it's in selling, speaking, teaching, litigating, negotiating, or managing.

You must aggressively and creatively develop Options that will facilitate your reaching your goal. And you'll be amazed at your ability to find these alternatives once you understand their value and commit yourself to finding them.

When the Critical Advisor appears after setbacks such as Pavin's shot at the Masters, you must again consciously react to your internal red flag and ask, "What are my Options?"

I explained all this to Critical Carl and he said, "Sounds great, but there are just too many situations in business where it is all or nothing, win or lose. In most situations there are no extra attractions or additional Options; there are only two doors. Then what I am supposed to do, make 'em up?"

Creative Options

"That's absolutely correct, Critical Carl. You must force yourself to be creative, to use your imagination." I was becoming animated because he had accidentally led himself to the answer. The reality, of course, is that there are always additional Options beyond complete success or abject failure. This is the fatal trap Polar Thinking sets for us.

Life is full of Options, perspectives, and interpretations, but Polar Thinking reduces our world to an either/or scenario that forces us into a room with just two doors—the two Options inherent in Polar Thinking.

After Corey Pavin put a ball in the water on the sixteenth hole, Polar Thinking and the Critical Advisor convinced him that there were no further Options. He felt he had walked through the door of failure. And, of course, he was wrong.

A Third Option Is Crucial

As Critical Carl pondered I said, "Keep in mind that the number of Options you develop is initially more important than the substance of those Options. And it's creating at least a third Option that cancels out the succeed-fail trap of two-option Polar Thinking."

The mind automatically tightens in a two-option scenario so the third Option brings a tremendous reduction in stress, anxiety, and fear. Those additional Options may appear to be frivolous, even ridiculous, but they provide your psyche with escape valves that are necessary.

Even a Stop-and-Go Light Has a Third Option

I said to Critical Carl, "Think of it like this. When your car approaches an intersection and the light is green, you know that before it turns red a yellow warning light will appear. What if they eliminated the yellow warning light?"

Critical Carl looked surprised and said, "You mean just have red or green, stop or go?"

"That's right," I replied. "What if there were just two lights?"

He laughed. "Well, to start with there would be a lot more accidents."

I nodded in agreement and added, "There would also be a great deal more tension and stress from drivers approaching the signal lights. The presence of a third light creates a fear-reducing alternative in exactly the same way a third action Option enhances your performance potential."

When you approach a stoplight at an intersection, you know it provides an Option in addition to stop or go. This reduces pressure in the same manner that having a third action Option does for you professionally.

Take a moment and picture yourself driving up to an intersection. The light is green as you get closer and closer. You know that you'll be caught in the middle if it suddenly switches to red. You're thinking, "Should I speed up? Wait, maybe I should slow down. No, I'll step on it and try to beat the light. Maybe I shouldn't. It's been green too long!"

Even on this small scale, you can feel a knot in your stomach as you imagine a stop-and-go light with only two Options. That stress, tension, and anxiety is magnified exponentially when you approach performance tasks with a Polar Thinking mentality.

Options Always Exist

I said to Critical Carl, "Whether you are giving a speech, are losing an important sale, are being denied a promotion, are facing diminishing returns in business, or anything else, there are always Options. You may give a speech in which your voice squeaks, your lips stick to your teeth, your mouth feels like it's full of cotton, and your jokes fall flat. As you walk away from the podium amid tepid applause, your Critical Advisor is waiting in the wings with a baseball bat ready to beat you up. Before that happens you have to create action Options other than failure that give you an action-oriented avenue to success."

"Like what?" Carl asked.

Happy to see his interest, I continued. "Like telling your-self that next time you are going to use a script," I responded.

"What if I used a script in the speech I just bombed with?" he countered.

"Then tell yourself next time you'll try working off notes with key topics listed and that you'll practice more and use the video at home to record and play back your performance, looking for ways to improve."

Critical Carl was making it difficult. "I haven't figured out how to get my video camera to work," he said.

"But," I interjected, "that Option exists and you can use it if you summon the interest. You can practice in front of your bathroom mirror! The point is that simply adminis-tering a self-bashing after a speech that was poorly received is completely counterproductive, just as it was self-destruc-tive for Corey Pavin to let himself sink into a daze when he blew that five-iron shot.

"Do you remember what I said about high achievers and the manner in which they respond to challenges? And recovering from tepid applause after a speech is certainly a challenge."

Critical Carl looked unsure. "Tell me again, Coach."

"Winners win," I continued, because they respond to setbacks by creating Options and by learning from the set-backs. San Francisco 49er Randy Cross did it in football but lost it in broadcasting until he learned to recognize the presence of Polar Thinking and his Critical Advisor and how to overcome them. Creating Options greatly assists in doing this." Critical Carl nodded.

"Remember how Bill Bradley suffered catcalls, verbal abuse, media derision, and public humiliation his first year in the NBA?" I asked.

Critical Carl smiled and said, "Gee, that was an amazing situation."

"Well, Bradley created Options for himself. He removed the public's Polar Thinking and Critical Advisor. He lifted the spell of perceived failure and began giving himself Options, which included playing strictly for the 'integrity' of the game, playing only for his teammates without concern for outside perceptions or expectations.

"Michael Jordan was asked if he gets nervous when the Bulls are down by a point with two seconds left in the game and he's got the last shot."

Critical Carl perked up. "What did he say?"

"Air Jordan believes he will make that clutch basket but also knows if he misses, 'there will always be another chance in another game.' Jordan is a master at presenting himself with a scenario where self-failure is absent because he finds Options. He says 'When you think about consequences, you always think of negative results.' Air Jordan avoids Polar Thinking by creating Options that enable him to stay in the Process."

In fact, Jordan recently told Ira Berkow of the *New York Times*, "I believe in myself at all times." Jordan believed in himself in 1995 when he returned to the Bulls and struggled through the season, and he believed in himself in 1996 when the Bulls ruled the basketball world. You can do the same and develop your ability to create action Options when the going gets tough.

Jordan has missed plenty of big shots, but somewhere along the way he removed Polar Thinking from his mentality. And remember, Jordan had to work at it. He was cut from the varsity squad when he was a sophomore in high school.

Super achievers have the ability to constantly create Options in a manner that gives them a psychological "exit" beyond failure and a practical avenue for achieving goals. However, something additional is required once you have created those action Options.

> *Learn from your mistakes.*
> —HAL LEONARD, orchestra conductor

As you create Options, it is equally important to simultaneously evaluate them as to merit and practicability and to reflect on them. You trigger this response with the second part of our two-part question.

"What Am I Learning from My Options?"

The newly created Options become valuable sources of information when you answer this important question, "What am I learning from my Options?"

If Pavin had asked himself this question on the sixteenth hole of the Masters, he would have initially Learned that he still had a chance to win the tournament even after his missed shot. Furthermore, in analyzing how to correct his mistake in preparation for the next shot, he would have developed a positive solution as he evaluated and Learned more. (For example: "I tried to steer the ball and it went in the water. I've got to remember to take a full backswing and then just swing through the ball. I'm pressing too hard.")

Restoring Self-Trust

By creating and then learning from Options, Pavin (or you) engages in something of great importance, which goes beyond simply acquiring the information produced by answering the question "What am I Learning?" Obviously, the Learning experience itself keeps you in the Process, involved in the moment and removed from Polar Thinking's anger, guilt, resentment, self-recrimination, dejection, or other negative feelings. It is positive and productive; it's solution oriented.

But equally valuable is the fact that Learning becomes a conduit to trusting your own judgment again after it has been beaten up by your Critical Advisor. This is very important because the Power of Hands-Free, the ability to perform up to your greatest potential, requires confidence in your judgment; that is, it requires self-trust. It is essential that you have self-trust to be in the Zone. That's how you managed to take your hands off of the handlebars as a kid. You trusted yourself. You believed!

The single biggest advantage of the Surge-Recover-Surge Game Plan is that it returns belief in your own judgment again. Learning is the key component in restoring that belief and self-trust.

To Notice and then create Options does little to restore your confidence and self-trust (although it does a magnificent job of destroying Polar Thinking and eliminating the Critical Advisor by giving you back control of the present, the Process). Learning takes those options and uses them constructively for regaining trust, belief, and confidence in yourself.

When you ask, "What am I Learning from my Options?" you start to restore self-trust, because in evaluating those options you are acknowledging subconsciously that you are in control. The Learning Process itself becomes self-empowering.

By engaging in the Process of drawing forth information and direction from the Options, you give yourself renewed inner strength. Thus, Learning becomes a very positive force because the moment you enter the Learning experience you quit judging yourself in the harsh perspective of the Critical Advisor and Polar Thinking. You are back in charge. You're positive and active rather than being a passive hostage to them.

Had Corey Pavin done this, it would have allowed him to break through his daze of emotion, his perceived failure, and get back among the living.

Rather than quitting he would have gone right back into the Process of trying to unleash his greatest potential. Instead the Process ended for him because Polar Thinking and the Critical Advisor took uncontested control.

When this daze happens it can deal a serious body blow to you or anyone else. It's often more than just stubbing your toe and can be psychologically and emotionally crippling. Getting back on course, back on your feet, requires a healing of your battered self-confidence. Learning from your Options provides this healing because you will Recover only when in your terms it makes sense to do so, and only when you come to your own conclusions.

Learning is the lever you can pull to allow yourself access to your own conclusions. And those conclusions are the foundation for once again trusting your judgment. Self-trust is a fundamental ingredient when it comes to unleashing your greatest potential.

Experience Plus Reflection Equals Wisdom

Experience plus reflection equals wisdom. And this is why winners can take setbacks and turn them to their advantage. Learning from experience, which includes reflecting on it (regardless of whether it's a positive or negative experience), creates wisdom. Wisdom is the foundation for confidence and self-trust. It is the muscle in the Recover process.

David Pottruck, president and COO of the Charles Schwab Corporation (with revenues over $1.4 billion), has put this equation to good use. He described during our conversations the change he has made in this regard. "Mistakes used to really shake me up. I would carry it with me, and it would shake my confidence. I would have a combination of self-doubt and self-recrimination. I would beat myself up. Now, I realize I'm going to make some mistakes. Part of being human is making mistakes."

Pottruck now *uses* the occasional mistake, setback, or failure instead of letting it use him. "All of us want wisdom, but how many of us take the time to be reflective? How many of us recognize the importance of this? And if we don't reflect [i.e., Learn] then we never go from experience to wisdom. We have this experience that gets stored in our brain, but without reflection I think the opportunity for wisdom, for judgment, for intuition, becomes limited. Experience plus reflection equals wisdom." Therein lies the key to self-trust, self-empowerment, and self-actualization.

Pottruck understands that only after you've Learned are you ready to proceed to the next and final question. It is the question that will put you back in the Power of Hands-Free.

RECOVER: DO DIFFERENTLY

(The Recovery Question)

Ask: What will I now Do Differently?

Critical Carl was making excellent progress in under-standing the Game Plan, and it was only a matter of time before he returned to his former level of productivity, con-fidence, and enthusiasm in his job.

Although he was somewhat challenged when it came to incorporating the Language of Inclusion into his internal and external dialogue (as it will also be for you), it was encouraging to note his success elsewhere. In fact, it was almost time to suggest a change in his nickname, but more on that in a moment.

"Critical Carl," I said, "having prepared for optimum performance with RVOC and then having gained a large measure of control, knowledge, and self-trust with the Notice and Options-Learning questions, there is still one final and decisive thing you must ask yourself to return into the Process of the Surge."

Critical Carl's sense of humor was intact. "Well, Coach," he answered, "I've got a tee time in one hour, but let's hear what you've got to say. Maybe it'll help my game."

I smiled and said, "I promise that it will help you in the game of golf and in the bigger game."

He shot back, "Hey, golf *is* the bigger game!"

I continued, "Critical Carl, as we have seen you can put a stranglehold on the Critical Advisor when you red flag it by asking, 'What am I Noticing?' When you have given consideration to that first question, you then remove Polar Thinking when you ask, 'What are my Options, and what am I Learning from them?' When you have answered this, it is time to set the stage for a return to the Power of Hands-Free."

The Final Question and Decision

"You set yourself up for reentry to the Surge by asking yourself this final performance question, 'What will I now

Do Differently?' That question narrows the focus on your Options. Having created, evaluated, and Learned from them—and in the Process having regained an increased level of self-trust—it is now time to choose to *Do* one of them. This is accomplished by asking and answering the final question, 'What will I now Do Differently?' "

"Coach, aren't you basically telling me that having created Options for myself, those additional exits you were talking about, that I've just gotta take a moment and pick the right Option?"

He had missed the nuance inherent in the question, so I explained further. "Critical Carl, an important element of this question is the wording. The question is 'What will I now Do *Differently*?' rather than 'How will I now do it right?' or 'What will I now do better?' The instant you say, 'What is the right Option?' or 'How will I do it right?' or words to that effect you have created a brand-new two-option Polar Thinking construct in which you ask, 'What Option is right . . . or wrong?'

"When you allow yourself the psychological comfort zone created by deciding simply what you will Do Differently, you make it extremely unlikely that the Critical Advisor will be aroused with issues of succeed-fail, right-wrong, or win-lose. You have taken Polar thinking out of play and greatly reduced the possibility that doubt, anxiety, and fear will reenter your perspective. It keeps you totally in the Process." He nodded with little enthusiasm.

My friend from Cleveland still had a lingering need to utilize the contest mentality of Polar Thinking. This is understandable because it's so deeply ingrained in all of us that it seems like the right thing to do, like the American Way. In fact, it is the American Way of doing things, even though it is frequently counterproductive.

"We are transfixed on the issue of how to do it right when, in fact, we should concern ourselves simply with just doing it. We need to break free from the enormous and debilitating pressure imposed by Polar Thinking."

Critical Carl was interested. "Got any examples?" he asked.

"Of course," I responded, "examples are my stock-in-trade." Here's how Jack Nicklaus asked "What will I now Do Differently?" after he created Options.

Nicklaus Does It Differently

During the 1989 PGA Championships at Kemper Lakes Golf Course at Hawthorne Woods, Illinois, Jack Nicklaus hit a powerful drive down the middle of the first fairway, almost three hundred yards. The crowd reacted with a burst of applause in appreciation of the Golden Bear's effort. On the fourth hole it was a different story, however. Again he boomed his drive off the tee, but this time it was a severe pull-hook that almost bounced out-of-bounds, as ugly a shot as Nicklaus is likely to hit. His reaction and subsequent decision is a wonderful example of how NOLD is put into action for optimum results.

In creating Options for himself, Nicklaus understood that he risked further damage if he continued to use his driver. It's the most volatile club in the golfer's bag (putter excepted), and even though its distance is highly valued, on tour Nicklaus was wondering if the pull-hook was evidence of a mechanical problem in his swing. Was there more trouble waiting if he used it again?

Nicklaus, perhaps the strongest mind in the history of golf, created Options and saw many: hit with the driver and hope for the best even though he now had doubt in his mind about it; hit with the more controllable three wood and lose perhaps fifteen yards or more in distance; hit with the four wood and lose thirty yards or more but increase control; or even, perhaps, hit with an iron (one or two) for a tremendous drop in distance but an equivalent increase in control. Factored into his decision about what to Do Differently was the fact that Kemper Lakes puts a premium on distance off the tee because the course is extremely long. A driver that is working well gives a player a significant advantage.

Jack Nicklaus saw many Options and Learned from them. In his own way he then decided what to Do Differently.

Critical Carl, a twenty-six handicapper at one of Cleveland's municipal golf courses, couldn't restrain himself. "The Bear stayed with his driver, didn't he? He didn't back off it early, did he?" I resisted mentioning my friend's exclusionary language because I was so pleased with his earlier modest success. Critical Carl said, "Then he must have gone with the three wood. It's safer, and Jack could still get good distance. He went to three wood, right?" I remained silent. "Coach, he didn't drop down to an iron, did he? I mean early in a round he wouldn't quit on himself, would he?"

I spoke up. "Critical Carl, you are missing the point. The real issue is the fact that over the years Nicklaus had become a master at creating Options for himself and learning from those Options. He avoided backing himself into a psychological corner where there were just two exits. In trying to Recover from a setback—a drastic pull-hook early in a round—he was able to offer himself various escape routes or Options and then decide what to Do Differently. That's what he was determining after the pull-hook."

I went on to explain to Carl that in his prime the Golden Bear had such competitive fortitude that he rarely was overwhelmed by negative emotions (à la Pavin and his daze) during a round. He had a magnificent ability to resist self-thrashing. Thus, he would immediately begin creating Options, Learning from them, and then quickly deciding what he would Do Differently. Thus, he was frequently in the Process of performance. He played with the Power of Hands-Free an inordinate amount of the time.

Instead of letting an early near-disaster cast a shadow of doubt over him, he red flagged it and made his choices. Essentially, he asked himself, "What are my Options, and what am I Learning from them?" and then he asked himself, "What will I now Do Differently?"

"Well, what did he decide to Do Differently?" Critical Carl inquired meekly.

"Three wood," I responded, "and he hit it great! And he also used the one iron on driving holes where the fairway was very tight and the penalty for an errant shot severe. And he kept the driver in his bag the rest of the day."

"Did he win the tournament?" my friend wanted to know.

"Critical Carl, you exhibit your obsession with Polar Thinking when all you care about is the win-lose result. The point of this story is Process and how to get back to it when trouble strikes or threatens to strike."

Jack Nicklaus was a formidable performer because he was able to get back to the Process so successfully. Payne Stewart won that tournament, but Nicklaus had successfully demonstrated his great mental management skills again, just as he had done so many times throughout his career.

Remember, although Jack Nicklaus has won more Majors than anyone in the world (twenty), he has also come in second more than anyone else (nineteen). Jack Nicklaus understands as well as anyone on the planet how to prepare, perform, and respond. He was a genius at the Process, of knowing how to Surge-Recover-Surge. It's one of the reasons he was the greatest clutch player ever.

And this obviously applies to business even more than golf. When the inevitable setbacks, roadblocks, and downturns occur, you will create Options and then determine what you will Do Differently.

Critical Carl's New Skills

"Critical Carl, you now have that same formula, a mental technology, to bring out your own best efforts under the tremendous pressures imposed in business. You have the tools to Surge on the Power of Hands-Free and then quickly Recover from setbacks and the Critical Advisor."

He looked at me with a confidence I had not seen that day. "I think I can almost finish this book for you now, Coach."

"Go head, I believe you can," I replied.

He continued, "Once I have decided the question 'What will I Do Differently?' I am once again ready to Surge with RVOC. The option I select is then ready to be put into action with RVOC, Ritualize, Visualize, Optimize, and Capitalize! It's circular—Surge-Recover-Surge."

I was very pleased. Critical Carl now understood how to incorporate the Game Plan for optimum performance into his profession and life on a consistent and continuing basis. "It's the secret for achieving successful performance results everywhere," I said, "because just as athletes face challenges and overcome obstacles and setbacks, you must do the same. The goal is to perform at your highest level, in the Zone, on a consistent basis. The Game Plan we have just shared together, the Principles of Surge-Recover-Surge, will allow you to do that. I promise."

"Guaranteed?" he asked with a smile.

"Guaranteed!" I replied, "as long as you apply what you have learned here in a conscientious manner, I promise you it will produce success and enjoyment. It will put you in the Zone on a regular basis."

Critical Carl smiled, pumped his fist, and shouted, "Yes!" He was back in the saddle.

UNLEASHING
YOUR OWN ZONE

We arrive now at the final pages in our journey toward unleashing our greatest potential both personally and professionally. One of the ways you can evaluate your progress is by noticing that you've traded in your badge of pain for a badge of enjoyment, enjoyment at being able to control Polar Thinking and the Critical Advisor.

Critical Carl and I began to conclude our conversation on a day that had been rainy but was becoming increasingly bright and sunny. I said to him, "Remember, the secret for obtaining your best personal results is to Surge, quickly Recover, and Surge. It means you will Surge with the Power of Hands-Free, Recover quickly when Polar Thinking summons up your Critical Advisor, and then Surge again with the Power of Hands-Free. You now have the formula that will allow you to successfully achieve that, RVOC for Surge and NOLD for Recover.

"Coach," he replied, "you make it sound like a beautiful, sunny day at the beach. I'm standing there in my baggy swimsuit, covered with Coppertone, and watching the seagulls swoop down over the ocean. Suddenly I see a huge rolling wave gathering tremendous power and force. I watch it crash into the beach and Surge up around my ankles. Then at a certain point it seems to falter. The ocean Surge stops flowing forward up the beach and begins to drain back out, almost like it's retreating into the sea gradually. As I stand there watching it, the wave appears to gather renewed strength, to Recover, and suddenly, there it is again, Surging back up onto the sand with its enormous force and power. Surge-Recover-Surge!"

Critical Carl from Cleveland had found a wonderful little metaphor for the entire process so common to men and women who are high achievers in business (and sports). He was absolutely right! Our performance ebbs and flows just like the ocean and just like the ocean, we have awesome power when we Surge on the Power of Hands-Free. We are powerful, confident, relaxed, and focused. We are in the Zone.

But when our performance ebbs and our self-trust, focus, and enjoyment retreat because Polar Thinking awakens our Critical Advisor, we must identify it just as clearly and quickly as when we see the ocean wave drawing back to the sea. Only then can we Recover quickly and return to our own personal Surge.

I told Carl, "Successful individuals in business know how to Surge-Recover-Surge, and now you have the same ability at your disposal. You, Critical Carl, have the Game Plan and the tools to unleash your greatest potential on a consistent and productive basis with RVOC and NOLD!"

Goodbye Critical Carl

"Coach, you make it sound almost like poetry," he replied.

I paused and then told him, "More than poetry, Critical Carl, it is power, the tremendous power you have within. That great potential is ready to be tapped again, to be utilized in achieving your goals. Most people never find a way to do that on a consistent basis. They go through their professional and personal lives like a hockey team with two players always in the penalty box. The sad part is they impose the penalty time on themselves. They put their own ability and potential in the penalty box without knowing that it is completely within their power to choose to operate at full strength."

"Hey, I like that penalty box bit, Coach," he replied. "That pretty well sums it up. Regardless of how much talent your team has, it will fall way short of reaching its greatest potential if guys are sitting on the bench doing penalty minutes. That's exactly what I've been doing to myself these last few years, sitting in the penalty box doing time imposed by Polar Thinking and my Critical Advisor. Those days are over. The penalty phase is over for me. I'm back at full strength!"

Critical Carl from Cleveland was actually a believer again, in himself and his abilities. That quality more than anything else identifies high achievers, those who prosper with both success and happiness.

The Michael Jordans, Steffi Grafs, Joe Montanas, Randy Crosses, Chris Everts, Pete Samprases, Kristi Yamaguchis, and John Woodens of this world have extremely positive attitudes about their efforts. It is an attitude you also have when you Surge on the Power of Hands-Free and Recover from Polar Thinking and your Critical Advisor.

"Critical Carl," I announced, "you are now back where you were as a child confidently riding a bicycle with your hands free and when you were at your best selling insurance. You are in the Zone with the Power of Hands-Free. You are back where you want to be, focused, full of self-trust, relaxed, and enjoying the Process.

"Equally important, you have the tools to Recover when Polar Thinking and your Critical Advisor jeopardize your performance potential. I believe it may be time we began addressing you by a different name. The Critical Carl I knew earlier is gone."

He smiled, knowing that what I told him was true. "Coach, that's a great idea. What do you think it could be? How about Confident Carl from Cleveland, or maybe Capitalizing Carl because I'm going to be Capitalizing on my strengths? Courageous Cal would be nice, or possibly Convincing Carl from Cleveland. Which one do you think is most appropriate?"

I paused. Turning toward him I realized they were all appropriate, that he was once again all of these and more.

"I believe we can drop the use of a nickname," I replied. "Let's go back to who you were at your very best, because that's who you are now. You are Carl. All the power and talent and drive exists within Carl, and you now have the knowledge, your own Game Plan, to summon forth this great potential, to surge on the Power of Hands-Free and be in the Zone."

He was moved. "Coach, you have given me back something that is very special. It is a gift that creates self-trust, belief, and enjoyment. It is the gift of being able to once again perform at my best."

We shook hands as he prepared to leave. I said, "Thank *you* Carl, and may the 'Hands-Free Zone' be with you!"

Then as he was opening the door to leave, he turned and looked back. With a confident smile he paused and asked, "Hey, Coach, it just occurred to me that I may be of great assistance to you when it comes to your life insurance policy. Tell me, what kind of coverage do you currently have?"

I had to chuckle. "Come on back here and sit down. I've been meaning to reevaluate my whole situation, and maybe the present time is good," I replied.

"The present is always good, Coach!" he replied. "The present is where the power is. The present is where the Zone is."

Yes, my friend Carl was where he belonged, back in the Zone.

AFTERWORD

The president and COO of the Charles Schwab Company,
David Pottruck, observed that success in sports or business results from a mental discipline and practice. Pottruck is correct. That mental discipline is what our book
provides, a formula for unleashing your best efforts. However, only with conscientious practice will *In the Zone* be
of benefit to you.

Many will read *In the Zone* and say, "Hey, this is great
stuff!" and then put it on their bookshelves where it will
gather dust. We promise those individuals that much of
what they have learned here will be soon forgotten.

While we can provide the Game Plan, you must provide
the practice. Reread our book again within fourteen days
and underline or highlight especially relevant ideas and
concepts. Discuss the ideas we present herein with associates, and look for immediate and specific applications in
your own profession (whether you are a salesperson, doc-

tor, manager, lawyer, coach, commercial artist, real estate developer, airline pilot, teacher, accountant, judge, claims adjuster, or other businessperson).

Then make a concerted effort to begin utilizing what we have presented just as you may have done as a young athlete who learned your team's game plan and then spent weeks practicing how to execute it in the game. The results today and in the future will be much more rewarding and significant.

Thirty days hence, go over your notes and highlighted passages again to refresh your thinking and motivate yourself.

Like any new and valuable skill, you must practice being in the Zone if you wish to have it become a part of you. Then and only then will you find yourself in the Zone time after time after time, whether you're a Critical Carl or a Critical Carla.

Good luck, and remember, you can do it!

May the "Hands-Free Zone" be with you—yes!

INDEX

ABOUT THE AUTHORS

Dr. J. Mitchell Perry

Dr. J. Mitchell Perry, president of the JM Perry Corporation in Palo Alto, California, is an award-winning organizational psychologist and entrepreneur who appears regularly on television and radio addressing issues of obtaining optimum performance results in business.

With a doctorate from the University of the Pacific, and formal training as a psychotherapist, Dr. Perry has grown JM Perry Corporation into an internationally renowed consulting and training company specializing in the creation of human leverage.

Perry is a regular keynote speaker at the National Entrepreneur of the Year Awards sponsored by *Inc. Magazine*, Ernst and Young, Merrill Lynch, *USA Today*, and NASDAQ. He is also a regular top-rated lecturer at the Wharton School of Business at the University of Pennsylvania. In addition he is frequently sought after by top business leaders around the world for his keen executive coaching skills.

Dr. Perry has been featured in the *Wall Street Journal*, *Success Magazine*, the *Los Angeles Times*, *Golf Digest*, the *San Francisco Chronicle*, *USA Today*, and many other regional and national magazines and newspapers. Among his many publications he has written a book entitled *The Road to Optimism: Change Your Language, Change Your Life*.

Dr. Perry resides in Stockton, California.

Steve Jamison

Steve Jamison is creator and coauthor of *Winning Ugly: Mental Warfare in Tennis*, one of the decade's most popular and highly acclaimed tennis books. It has been published in Germany, Japan, Austria, and Switzerland.

A keynote speaker, Jamison addresses the sports-life connection in his seminars and public appearances. He is president of Winning Ugly, Inc., in San Francisco, California, a company which also publishes the Winning Ugly Sports Calendar and produces other Winning Ugly products for golf, tennis, and other sports.

Jamison's work has appeared in the *Chicago Tribune*, the *San Francisco Examiner*, the *Minneapolis Tribune*, *Golf*, *Tennis*, *Men's Health*, the *San Francisco Chronicle*, and many other publications. His most recent book is *Wooden: A Lifetime of Observations and Reflections On and Off the Court*, written with legendary UCLA basketball coach John Wooden.